Black Coal Into Diamonds!

Touching Stories from WW II era:

"Lure of the 82nd Airborne"

*"Rumblings of the Thunderbirds
in the 42nd Division"*

"Diamonds from the Mines of Manhattan"

W9-BEK-804

with many other "stranger than fiction" stories!
—J. Robert Boggs, Editor

Dedication

To all the brave men and women
who have gone abroad
and
all those who have
"stayed by the stuff" at home
and have still given their time, talents
and their very lives
in the <u>service</u> of human freedom—
political and/or spiritual
for us all
we humbly and lovingly
dedicate this book.

Published by:

Boggs Books

John R. & Jodie Boggs
1408 Camelot Dr.
Winona Lake, IN 46590
Toll-Free: 877-292-2122

ISBN 0-9648880-0-9

Library of Congress Control Number: 2002096047

Acknowledgments

Yes, "I am debtor" to my dear and faithful wife, Jodie; our big, loving family; to our many friends, especially to those who have taken the time to respond to my request for a story. Many are busy people with things on their agenda besides taking time to write or tell a story to an old guy who doesn't *seem* as busy as they are! To my dear friend and banker, Al Disbro (Lake City Bank, Warsaw/Winona Lake, IN) who "worked like a trooper" on the picture for the front cover; to my new FL friend, Jn. D. Miller, along with Jim Grau, who helped fix many problems with this temperamental computer; *I thank you all and so many more!*

My sisters, Robbie and husband, J. T. Garrett; Martha and husband, Oren Schaffer; my niece, Ruth and husband, Wm. Mercer Massengale, (who seems like my blood-brother.) And he acts just like one (a better brother I couldn't imagine!) I love him like one of my ten sisters who have always been so very "special" to me, and made me feel rich, even without "blood" brothers. I've often said that the blood Jesus shed for us makes all believers "blood kin" anyway. I have long been indebted to my niece, Kathleen and her husband, Howard Alley, for their love, help and encouragement. He has just written an excellent historical novel *"Presumed Dead-A Civil War Mystery"* which is a "must read" for all who love our country and appreciate the struggles God has brought us through to get us to this place in our history where trusting and obeying God is an *absolute necessity* for us to make it through the grave perils we now face in 2003! Thank God for wanting to save all *the world he "so loved"!*

THANK YOU ALL!—J. R. B.

Introduction

Geologists tell us that diamonds are made from lumps of coal under great pressure and heat deep in the bosom of the earth.

Personal observation has led me to the conviction that most people who contribute much to their world are tested under great pressures.

Many exemplary people I know or have read about go through the fires of tests and obstacles they have to overcome. They not only survive but they also bless, lift and encourage others whose lives they touch. I know of few exceptions. Some live to be old, while others die young. These seemingly "extraordinary" people not only overcome obstacles and reverses; they also inspire faith in other people to believe they too can win—some having severe difficulties to overcome.

Many face some form of "deficit" early in life. Nevertheless they do not allow handicaps to speak the final word! They learn to deal with deficits. From somewhere deep inside them they embrace an optimism that, I believe, the great Creator puts in each of us! They fan that spark of inner faith that becomes for them an asset of an outward, objective reality. They could make excuses/alibis like most people do, but instead they choose the path of obedience to and trusting in the God of grace and love.

Take a look at a few *sparkling diamonds* I have found along the path! These plain, ordinary people *effectively used their power of choice.*

Confronted by the pressures of poverty, the devastation of divorce, or deluged by diseases like Alzheimer's or cancer, they cling to hope. Many who start with severe limitations in talents/abilities *or* later are surprised by accidents, social/financial reverses, untimely death in the family, or . . . ? But these profound optimists never give in, give up or quit. They deliberately choose to believe they can "overcome." I call them *"In spite of"* people.

May their examples inspire you to believe that you too, can be a winner in life's race, in spite of . . . !

—J. Robert Boggs

Contents

1

Lure of the 82ⁿᵈ Airborne

Part 1

—RUTH MASSENGALE

THE YEAR was 1940. We lived in Atlanta, Georgia, almost in sight of the gold dome of the capitol building. I was 16 years old.

I planned to visit my great grandmother, Sarah Posey, 50 miles west, near Bremen, so my friend Dorothy and I went down the street to a Rogers market to buy her a box of candy. We had no supermarkets in those days, but a store where we were each waited on personally. No buying loads of things, but just what we needed at the moment, with what money we had. We had no freezer, or way to keep foods for long. We did have a wooden ice box that helped. A man came every day or two with a big block of ice on his padded shoulder to replace the one that was usually melted to a sliver.

With a quarter in my hand, we went over to the counter to get a box of chocolate-covered cherries. Laughing and giggling, we observed the handsome boy with black wavy hair—and a big smile—behind the counter, ready to wait on us. I noticed that he kept smiling at me, which both delighted me and made me blush at the same time. We all considered *Dot* the pretty one, and would have expected it if a boy flirted with her. But me? It kinda' took me off guard. Soon it was plain that his attention was on *me!*

I nervously gave him the quarter and took the box of candy. He must have been nervous too, because he dropped the quarter I gave him—well, one of us did—and it fell into a crack in the old counter!

"Oh!" I exclaimed. "That was the only quarter I had with me, and I wanted to give the candy to my grandmother. Now what will I do?"

"Don't worry about it! I'll find it. It's down in that crack," he reassured me. He kept smiling at me until we were out the door. Years later he told me that he confided in his boss afterwards: "I'm gonna' marry that little girl some day. Who is she, anyway? Do you know her?"

"Yes, I know her. She and her mother live close by—and yes, I'm confident she will be back."

That week-end my mother and I traveled 50 miles west to visit my grandma and great grandma. In my young heart I was hoping that handsome guy would be in that store the next week when I came back—and he was! I had remarked to Dot after we left that day, "Wow! He's so cute!"

"I think he likes you," said my friend Dot. "He surely was smiling at you." The name of the handsome youth with a million-dollar smile: William Mercer Massengale, from Starr's Mill, near Brooks and Peachtree City, Georgia.

The next week we needed a loaf of bread or something. With delight I went to the store. There he was! I asked him, "Did you find that quarter we lost last week?"

"Oh, yes, I found it!" So began our courtship, as we *found each other* while looking for a lost coin. We also found a very sweet 60 year relationship over a box of candy—and a quarter that fell into a crack!

Dot and I went often to that store. If we each had a nickel for a candy bar—they had a three for a dime deal—one of us would take both nickels and buy three candy bars and cut the extra one in two. It was an early lesson in cooperation and human togetherness. We were always thinking up excuses to go to the store, and the candy bargain was one of the "sweet" excuses.

One day as I handed him the two nickels he took my hand and sorta' squeezed it. If I happened to go in when he was working in the back of the store, my heart would sink if I left without that beautiful smile from "Bill." But he and his boss, Mr. Ford, found a way to remedy that. "When she comes in, if I'm working in the back, would you please alert me, boss?" Mr. Ford was delighted to do just that. He was probably re-living his own early romantic adventures as he would playfully say, in a loud whisper, "Hey, Bill! Here she comes! Find something to do up front quickly."

Bill said the first time he saw me I was wearing a plaid skirt, skating on the sidewalk, coming to the store.

As our friendship developed, our "trust level" grew. One day when St. Valentine's Day was coming up, Bill said, "Could I ask you somethin'?"

"Sure. What?" I said.

"Could I have a date with you tonight?" I felt my face flush.

"I don't date!" I said. My mamma wouldn't let me. She would *not* let me out with you!"

"Does your mamma come to this store?"

"Yes, why?"

"Well, I'm gonna' ask *her* if I can have a date with you."

"You go right ahead," I said, "but you don't know my mamma! She won't let me date." (I must say that she let me be with boys in a group, or sit with one at a show in a group. But she did *not* let me "go out" at that age.)

One day Mr. Ford saw mother coming toward the store and he said to Bill, "Here comes Ruth's mother, O.K.?" Whereupon Bill walks over to her, introduces himself, and then tells her that he would like to date her daughter.

"Mamma Jewel" minced no words! "I don't let my daughter go with boys. She's too young. She's only 16.

No, I don't let her go out with boys, especially in cars. Besides, you're too old for her."

"Well, Ma'am, I'm only 19."

By then "Mamma Jewell" had taken time to scrutinize this handsome young fellow with such innocent looking brown eyes and friendly smile. So she said: "Well, I won't let her go *anywhere* on a school night, but if you want to come *down to the house* and see her some *other* night, you may."

That was the only encouragement young Bill needed. He came down that very night. Then on St. Valentine's night he came again, and brought me a great big box of candy.

His parents lived in Fayetteville and it wasn't too long before he wanted to take me thirty miles south to meet his family. I had turned 17 and my mother thought it was all right if he took me to meet his family. No sooner had we arrived in Fayetteville than we saw a 12-year old boy riding a bicycle and he said, "That's my brother going there." I met his mother, who I later learned was going to have a baby. I didn't even know it—he never told me or mentioned it once! I also met a sister who was my age. She was very possessive of her big brother, and did not look kindly on the idea of sharing his attention with another girl, especially one her age—and not even from Fayetteville!

When Bill shared with his parents his future marriage hopes, his dad said, "Well, you're almost 21, and I can't tell you what to do. I just hope you know what you're gettin' into."

Bill gave me a ring on my 17th birthday, and let me know he would like to get married in the not-too-distant future. My response was, "Oh, law! If I even mentioned marriage to Mamma, she would kill me! Well, no. Not really. She would die herself!"

In his cute southern drawl, Bill responded: "Well, I'm gonna' go talk to your mamma, and I'll ask her if it would be all right for me to marry her daughter." How was *that* for self-confidence!

I said, "Well, I don't want to be anywhere near when you ask her!" That was in August. You would have had to know my mother, "Mamma Jewel", to appreciate the fact that I took off to spend two weeks in west Georgia at the farm with my grandma—fifty miles away from the most handsome fellow I had ever known—just to be sure that I was not even *close* to Atlanta when Bill asked if it would be "all right" for him to marry her 17-year-old daughter! We all laugh hilariously about it now, but back then . . . !

I finally got a welcomed letter from Bill in which he said, among the more romantic things: "I went to see your mother. She cried but she said she knew I would make you a good husband; she knows I love you, and she knows that you love me. Then she gave me her permission. She broke down and cried a long while. So, my darling, the coast is clear!"

Well, that was *good* news! I felt it was safe to go back home now—just as soon as Garland, who was working in Atlanta, came to see Connie again, so I could ride back with him. We'll skip all the beautiful moments and romantic encounters from August to December 7, 1941. That day Bill came to get me at my cousin's (the Dixon's) on Bolton Road and we headed to his folks at Fayetteville south of the Atlanta airport, to spend the day, and enjoy Mrs. Massengale's "superb" home-cooked food, and to update the family on our hopes and plans to get married around Christmas time. We walked in and "Dad" Massengale met us, looking pale and teary-eyed. Seeing him like this told us us immediately that a devastating tragedy of some kind had struck. "Well, we're in war," he said, with trembling voice. Pointing to the radio, he continued: "President Roosevelt is still on the radio. He said the Japanese have bombed Pearl Harbor, and we have declared war. You know what that means."

Suddenly our beautiful, warm, romantic world turned to a bleak, cold, dark and foreboding landscape. The "eighteen days before Christmas" spirit of celebration quickly turned to sobs that could be heard all around the living room. No one needed to say it, but we all knew the healthy young men in their late teens and early twenties would be the first to be called up in a draft we felt sure would come. The heart of each of us turned toward our bright, handsome *William Mercer Massengale.* We all wanted to yell:

"No! You can't take *him* from us! Please try to find another way!" Knowing that we were only one family among thousands suddenly caught in this gut-twisting experience on that same fateful day didn't seem to help a lot at the moment. The grief of the nation was suddenly *personal*—and the devastating hurt was deep inside each of us, and very real, even though in a sense it seemed ethereal. It was like a terrible dream from which you hope to awaken, discovering it was only a dream. The terrifying part of it was that we all knew it was not a dream—that we would eventually have to start, as best we could, to cope with a new set of circumstances or reality.

After tearful good-byes, Bill and Ruth finally tore themselves away to head back to Atlanta. For quite a while they rode along in stunned silence, like thousands of other lovers throughout America on that special December 7. Finally, Bill spoke up and said: "Wednesday is my day off at the store. Let's get married then. We both know that within a year I'll be drafted and I'd like for us to be together every day we can until then."

"That doesn't give us much time to get ready," I quickly rejoined.

"I don't care. I want us to have all the beautiful experience of married life we possibly can until I have to leave you. There's no time to plan a big wedding. I've heard that lots of young couples who get married go down to the old guy who is the "Ordinary" at Conyers, Georgia, not far away. We can get our license tomorrow and have him marry us Wednesday night."

Can you imagine Mother's state of shock when I got home and told her we were getting married in three days?

We didn't have a long time of preparation for our wedding but Bill got a couple who boarded where he did in Atlanta to stand up with him. I got my best friend, Dot, to stand up with me as we prepared to head down to Conyers. Mother didn't want to go but Bill turned on his best "powers of charm and persuasion" and she finally said: "Well, where's my coat. You're gonna' get married anyway, so I may as well go." She cried all the way there, which was predictable for her.

It was getting late when we finally found the Ordinary's house and knocked on the door. He was already in bed, but his wife got him up. He came out with his sock nightcap still on! He took one look at me and said, "You can't get married. You're too young. You're still just a child!"

"I'm seventeen," I said.

"Maybe so. But you can only get married in Georgia at that age with a parent's consent!"

"Well, I have my mother here!"

He looked at my blond 35-year-old mother and scornfully retorted: "*She's* not your mother!" Then he noticed that she showed signs of having shed lots of tears—and was still close to tears—so he changed his mind. "Well, maybe she is your mother. All right, sign this paper over here."

William Mercer Massengale and Ruth Davis were married on December 10, 1941, at the home of the "Ordinary" in Conyers, Georgia, with only a few witnesses—along with who knows how many of heaven's angels and with cupid leading the choir!

Bill was right! We did have one full year of happy married life together before he had to leave for the armed services. Starting without a house/furniture or "nest egg" had its difficulties, but he had a job, worked hard, and we had true love. We loved our Lord; we loved each other and our country. That was the mortar that held life together for us and, I'm sure, for many others like us. And, would you believe, just nine months and ten days after what we now consider our sweet but hilarious wedding, God did visit us with an ever-giving "bundle of joy" when our little doll, Donna, arrived. We are still grateful to the draft board for giving Bill a three-month deferment from the draft to enjoy his first-born a while before joining thousands of others to help stop just one more egotistical mad man from his hell-bent plan to enslave people and murder many millions more! (Did you ever try to estimate what just one of these "mad men" costs our world, without trying to figure the cost of all of them in history? Think of the big savings in dollars and lives if they were stopped **earlier** on their sinister plots! *Editor*)

*   *   *

Bill's three-month deferment was up in December of 1942, just a few days before Christmas. Gratitude for those three crucial months kept him from asking any more favors. With a breaking heart, he kissed tiny Donna and me good-bye and boarded the street car in front of our little apartment just south of the capitol in Atlanta. He reported to the draft board and they sent him immediately over to Fort MacPherson, there in Atlanta.

Can you imagine my emotions while sitting alone all day on Christmas with little three-month-old Donna? No car or telephone; just the two of us in the quietness of a little sparsely furnished apartment in the big city of Atlanta. No Christmas decorations or any festive thing to speak of the "Prince of Peace" born on December 25!

But I did have plenty of formula for little Donna, plus cans of corn, beans, etc., for myself on the pantry shelf. Soup and crackers can be real tasty when you get hungry enough! When a holiday—or any special day—brings a surprising turn of events you're not prepared for, you still have choices to make. You can think of other people in the world who, at that moment, are in much worse circumstances than you and pray for them. Or you can think only of yourself and what you had hoped and planned and have yourself a first-class pity party. You can "curse your fate" or take a quick inventory and decide to make the most of what you have.

Bill, my young husband at "Ft. Mac," was not allowed to come the short distance home, even for a few hours. Had they known all this, someone in his family or mine would surely have come. The old saying, "ignorance is bliss" again proved very false.

But wait! All is not lost! On that dark Christmas night my young, resourceful husband, Bill, called the next door neighbor and had her get me to come to the telephone. "I've found another draftee who lives only two miles from us over by Grant's Park. His wife is coming to Ft. Mac! Her husband called and asked her to stop by and bring you with her! She'll come by there to pick you up about 7:30!"

To this message I responded: "But what will I do with the baby? It's cold and windy—and raining!" Bill said: "Get Mrs. McClain to come over and stay with her. She'll be glad to do it. It may be a long time before we see each other again." Eighty-five year old Mrs. McClain was more than glad to make herself useful to her two young neighbors and it worked out perfectly! And surely enough the young potential hero-soldiers shipped out the next morning to "destination unknown" which turned out to be Ft. McClelland over in Alabama. Yes, it was some time before I saw Bill again.

On that bone-chilling Atlanta Christmas night, two fellows eagerly looked for the right sedan to drive up with their young women who were their "special treasures." The time with us out there in the old Chevvy was not long, but the sweet savor of those moments still lingers in the memory of at least two of the four grateful souls now in our early 80's.

What I lacked in preparation of Christmas dessert was well taken care of by our new-found friends with a car. She had a big box of cakes, etc., beyond my wildest dreams! The four of us shared hugs, kisses and Christmas desserts. Typically, Bill had one last big piece of cake he was "too full to eat." He wrapped it up and said to me, "You take this home and eat it later. Give my little 'Donna-Doll' a tiny bite of it and tell her I will love her forever."

Then "taps" signaled the painful parting of many young Atlanta couples.

This was the first of a long list of "providential provisions" the Great Creator/Sustainer of the universe did under the grateful observation of William Mercer. The years he spent in the service of God and country were highlighted by incidents some would call "coincidences" but he would say, "They were God's providential leadings and provisions, and some were outright miracles."

Letters from young "Private Massengale" came with welcomed regularity. One Saturday night, about midnight, I answered the door and there stood handsome young Bill in his Army uniform! With a weekend pass, he got a bus to Atlanta and came "out home" on the street car! What a happy few hours! That was one of the little "Oases" in the 13-week basic training at "Ft. Mc" over in Alabama.

Near the end of week 13, Donna and I were down at Bill's folks in Fayetteville. We had just sat down to eat supper and a neighbor came over. "You have a message on the telephone." It was Bill!

"We're shipping out Monday morning and I don't know where. Get someone to keep the baby and come this weekend. Ride the bus and I'll be out in front of 'Ft. Mc' where the bus stops." I went. As it turned out, this time *was* the last time I was to see him for almost three years!"

Alabama to Pennsylvania

Bill's next contact was a telephone call from a fort in Pennsylvania—Camp "Shenago" or some such name. He got my hopes up a bit by saying: "If I should by any chance get stationed here, I could move you and Donna up and we would be together even while I'm serving our country."

But he was a dreamer! And so was I, to allow myself to even think momentarily of being together again so soon. The loneliness of a quick change from the joy and security of a husband who took charge of every situation we had to face in our first year of marriage to living alone in a small, cramped-up apartment with a baby to care for was enough to make a young bride wonder if she had been a bit looney a year ago. To add to my problems, we suddenly went from the security of a steady paycheck to a big fat "0" income. Speaking of earnings, we had both been brought up to pay our bills. Nine months and ten days is not enough time to save the needed money for doctor and hospital bills that happen when you have a baby! We were still doing our best to get them paid when Bill suddenly was taken from his family and job to sacrifice himself on the altar of freedom.

It was expected that we should give the Army thirty days to get the paper work done and the support checks started to sustain those left on the home front. But three months? And not one word of any kind from "Uncle Sam." This is the kind of situation where you need the anchor of a Higher Power in your life and rearing to help see you through!

We survived the three months without my husband-provider, but I can tell you that each month seemed like a year! Much has been spoken/written about the importance of letters to our service people when they are away. The case cannot be overstated. Many a life has been destroyed overseas—not by the deadly weapons of the foes they face—but by a "Dear John" letter from an unfaithful mate back home. My husband could probably say a word about that from his observation. A strong word should also be said for the importance of the total support for those left back home by family and friends as well as our government. I'm not bitter about it but I still have three month's wife and child support that the U.S. Army has never sent me from World War II! They seemed to think that because paper work from Forts in Georgia and Alabama didn't catch up for three months, the whole thing should just be forgotten. I forgave, but the pain of it was too real to ever forget! Someone said we should still try to collect it—with interest! My husband might be embarrassed that I even remember it but it happened. Small as the allotment was, it would surely have helped a lot back in the early 40's.

The war was heating up and only the necessary numbers of men were kept in the staging areas in the states. All the rest were shipped overseas as soon as they were deemed ready for the rigors that awaited them as they stepped ashore on the other side of the "pond" as many of them called it.

Before I let my dear husband, Bill, tell his side of our story, I want to share with you one more agonizing moment. I had not heard from him in what seemed like a l-o-n-g time. Here came a letter postmarked "APO, New York, N.Y."

"Goody! They have moved him again. Now he's in New York. No wonder I didn't hear from him for a while!"

My neighbor lady looked at the letter and said hesitantly, "I hate to tell you but he is on his way overseas. APO stands for 'Army Post Office.' They put that on letters that come *from* and *go* to overseas." It took a long minute for the truth of what she said to soak in but when it did, I began to weep almost uncontrollably and lash out at our fate.

That broke my heart! "Do you mean to say he's going overseas? Don't tell me that! I'll never see him again! He'll be killed! What are they doing sending him overseas to the front lines? He had only thirteen weeks of training!" So played out my reaction to the news while my helpless neighbor listened and wondered what words to say that might be a comfort. She didn't say much but she was always there for me. It seems that young people like us need a word of kindness and wisdom often. Reminds me of the little poem I ran across recently:

> *It was only a kindly word,*
> *And a word that was lightly spoken,*
> *Yet not in vain for it stilled the pain*
> *Of a heart that was nearly broken.*
>
> —*Anon*

I'll never forget the kindnesses of this 85-year-old neighbor. During the three months I eagerly waited for that first allotment check from the Army, her lovely daughter brought her a delicious, nutritious supper every evening—a really complete meal. Not long after the daughter would leave, here came my dear neighbor with a plate of good food saying, "Ruth, honey, my daughter brought me so much food I couldn't eat it all. Could you eat the rest of this? I hate to throw it out." I had to swallow my pride to accept it but I did, and I've been so glad I humbled myself to be a gracious receiver who did not cheat her out of the blessing of giving! Sharing blessed her, while helping me over a very rough spot in life's road. She must have been an excellent cook in her day, for her daughter certainly was! Before long I began to think her mom had told her of my plight, because the portions she brought seemed to gradually get larger. Not only had she taught her daughter to cook; she taught her compassion for fellow humans in embarrassing and needy situations.

With overarching anxiety, months dragged slowly that first lonely year, punctuated by the jubilation of letters and a few phone calls at first.

When our families discovered my plight, they were loyal to help every way they could. My Grandmother Boggs came and stayed a while with me. I remember how she "went to bat" for me when the appliance store was about ready to repossess my kitchen stove during those first three months! She "told them off" in no uncertain terms and paid the last $10 on it herself! (The Georgia legislature passed a law making it illegal to harass or push any service man's family for debts until he was home again.) She had the baby and me come out to the farm near Bremen for extended visits, too.

When the war dragged on for a few years, I was able to get a lady to stay with little Donna so I could work at the Office of Price Administration (O.P.A.) government office in Atlanta. They paid good wages but that nice job had its down side. It cost almost half of my paycheck for babysitters who were not always trustworthy. (Like favorite jewelry missing. Once I came home to find no baby or maid! After hours of sheer *terror,* we found baby, maid and her boy friend out drinking/driving!)

Eventually, I could not take this lack of integrity and went to my boss at the O.P.A. to resign my job. I was that "fed up." The boss said, "It's only two months until Donna will be two years old and she can then be left in the nursery. Why not just take a leave of absence until then and you can come back and go to work?" So that's exactly what I did. I had to carry the baby six blocks every morning to the nursery on the way to work but I was later glad I did. Finally, I had enough money saved to buy me a little house in Atlanta. I took my $1,000 down payment to sign for the house—only to discover that I had to be 21! My mother had to stay off work one day to go and sign for me. The little white house seemed like a mansion to me compared to the small apartment where the landlady only turned the hot water on one day a week. (That was the day we all took a bath!) But thankfully, my husband came home to a wife, a three-year-old daughter, and a cute little white house!

Finally, the war was over and the nightmare turned into a "homecoming supreme" for many of our husbands. The really sad part was the lives/homes permanently destroyed on both sides. My husband returned with honors to run a café. He later developed a good real estate business. His honesty and hard work paid off really well.

Beyond financial success, we count our greatest blessings in personal terms: Our three-year-old Donna was joined by three brothers to enlarge our family after the war! All four of them have embraced the Christian faith and come to beautiful maturity in it. We came to see and feel the supreme value of that blessing when our oldest son, Melvin, was brutally murdered while working for an Atlanta bank in the automatic teller machine department. I tell you, God's arms were literally underneath us in that agony and sorrow. That was fifteen years ago. Many injustices will have to await the real settlement on God's final Judgment Day!

Tom Brokaw has called ours "The Greatest Generation." Many of us are afraid he's right, though we still pray and cling to our hope for this one! Our children and grandchildren are in it! Millions of us are hoping/fervently praying for a spiritual renewal in our nation that will turn aside God's wrath and judgment and allow him to bless us instead. It is our decision, not God's, to make. We know he is eager to save and bless us! I refuse to give up—yet.

But we all know deep inside us that to have God's favor we must turn from the evil of our ways and start to think and live *right*. I believe it's that simple—and important.

I'm glad to tell my side of the World War II story, Mr. Brokaw—from the viewpoint of a 17-year-old girl, wife and mother! It's told now from the heart of a caring grandmother who loves her family very much—one who also believes God does not "play games" with nations or individuals. I hope what I have had to say will not only renew memories in many of you who are older but will arouse within each of us the spirit of *thankfulness*.

Now let me introduce you to a guy I've been married to more than 60 years! He earned the rare reputation of being "the most honest real estate dealer in Atlanta." I have been proud of him and happy to be his wife and the mother of his four children. Please read on. . . .

Lure of the 82nd Airborne

Part 2

WILLIAM MERCER MASSENGALE
(*As told to J. Robert Boggs,* Editor)

WELL, RUTH HAD IT pretty close to right, so I'll just add a little to the story for "color." When my daddy came to the door on December 7, 1941, in Fayetteville, Georgia, he was trembling badly and almost white as a sheet My mother had made a big chocolate cake. It was there on the table—the kind that Ruth could usually hardly wait to get a big piece of—but it had not been cut!

After President Roosevelt had finished his radio speech, and almost everyone had sniffled and sobbed about half an hour, I said, "Ruth, let's cut us a piece of that cake."

She reached for another Kleenex to blot the mascara that was getting smeared down her face and said tearfully, "No, thanks. I'm not hungry. I feel a little sick, even."

"What's the matta' with you all! You're actin' like someone had died already! Don't you think the Good Lord knows how to take care of a guy in th' Army? Besides, nobody had said anything about a draft. Maybe there'll be enough volunteers without a draft. I think I feel as bad about this thing as anybody, but God hasn't died! Cheer up, folks, and let's get on with our lives! We've gotta' take a day at a time!"

Truthfully, inside I was sorta' shook up, too. I had kind of an eerie feeling at our president's declaration of war but I chose to act like I thought the oldest son in the Massengale family ought to react, and let our talk be mixed with a little of our good Baptist Christian theology. I did—and do believe—that the Almighty God *was* and *is* in charge of everything and that if He permitted anything to happen, *He would* see us through it all!

After trying to eat a little to keep us going, Ruth and I gave each of my family a hug and headed 30 miles toward Atlanta. Ruth says *I* suggested we get married right away, but my version is that *she* suggested it! Does a small difference like that sound familiar? The truth was we *both* were so much in love with each other that we wanted to be married and together face the future. That's what we did—starting real soon after December 7, 1941! The "Ordinary" at Conyers, Georgia, was Sam Morris. "Marrying Sam," they called him, for the obvious reason. One thing I'll never forget is his long stocking nightcap he was still wearing when he came into the living room for the wedding! He took it off and laid it on the couch and proceeded. When it was all over I asked him how much I owed him. Here's how I recall his reply: "Young man, I usually charge $3.00, but in your case I"ll only charge you $1.00." I quickly took out a $1.00 bill and gladly paid him. I was making $8.00 a week where I worked. The going wage was $1.00 a day in those days, so I must have been worth a little more than average! I usually did two days worth of work on Saturday, so it was really seven days worth of work for $8.00

Anyway, I was glad for the bargain I got in the marriage ceremony! I've always figured I got a real bargain in every way when I got Ruth for a wife, and have told her many times that only she and I together, of all earth's people, could have united our genes and chromosomes to bring into the world these four particular quality children God gave us.

Ruth has told you about the trauma of my having to leave her and Donna just a few days before Christmas in 1942. When they shipped the big bunch of us to Ft. McClellan in our neighboring state of Alabama, they kept us so busy in basic army training that I didn't have time to get lonesome. But to say I missed my precious wife and daughter was a gross under—statement. But I was caught up in the great cause of "saving the world's freedom." And I still think it was a truly great cause. What *if* we had not done it???

With my background as a meat cutter in a grocery store, I got into a cooking and baking school after basic was over. The captain must have been impressed with my ability. He wanted to keep me there in Ft. McClellan and make me a mess sergeant. Orders from higher up came to send on all able-bodied men in class 1-A after their basic training.

With that in mind the captain sent me to a doctor (who was a major) for a new physical. The doctor said: "Private Massengale, your captain wants to keep you here to work for him. All we need to do is put a bar of soap under your arm for a certain length of time and take your blood pressure again, and you won't be shipping out anywhere. You'll be stationed right here in good ole' Alabama for the duration."

I said, "Major, I don't participate in things like that. I hate to disappoint anyone, but I can't go along with it. Back in Atlanta my boss at Rogers Markets wanted me to fill out a bunch of papers to get a deferment as a 'food handler' so I wouldn't have to leave Atlanta, and I wouldn't do it. I told him I was a patriotic boy who loved my country and wanted to do anything for it that I could, and I didn't consider myself better than the rest."

So they put me on the troop train headed north. They didn't give me any papers or anything. My commandant said, "I'm giving you a bunch of men to help you, so get on that troop train and feed the men on their way."

I did, and we ended up some days later in Camp Shenango, Pennsylvania. When they called the name of each man, he walked down the steps. Finally, I was the only one left and they never called my name. I figured that they meant for me to go back to Alabama on the train and feed another bunch on the way north. I asked the conductor of the train and he said: "This train isn't going back to Alabama. This is the end of the line."

I followed the crowd to the bunk houses and found an empty bunk to sleep in. Everybody had papers with orders except me. In a few days I was well rested and getting bored with nothing to do. Soon this bunch of men shipped out and others came in. This seemed to be sort of a staging area of some kind. One day I wandered over to the mess hall and began to talk with the fellow in charge of the meat department in the kitchen. I told him they apparently had lost my papers and I wondered if they needed any help there in the kitchen. "What did you do in civilian life?" he asked.

"I was a meat cutter in a grocery store, sir" I said.

"Do you know how to bone meat?" he asked.

"Yes, sir," I replied. Then he took me into the kitchen cooler, got me an apron and hat, and showed me the biggest pile of meat I had ever seen.

"Would you like to bone this meat?"

"I'd be happy to, sir." He left and I set to work.

Several hours later I finished boning the meat and cutting it into strips like he suggested, and I wandered outside and found the fellow. "Sir, I'm finished with th' meat."

"You're kidding me. You couldn't be!" he said.

"Sir, I'm finished," was my response. We walked into the kitchen and he was amazed at the big pile of bones in one place and a giant pile of meat strips in another place. He put his arm around my shoulder and said, "I'm gonna' keep you!" I worked there about a week with him.

One day the mess officer came in, walked up to me and asked, "Who are you?"

"I'm Bill Massengale, sir. I came in on a troop train some time ago. They seem to have lost my papers. Nobody seems to have my record."

Well, I'm sorry, but you can't stay here," he finally said.

"Sir, what am I supposed to do?" I said. After some thought he said:

"I'll tell you what to do. I'm gonna' tell the officer to put you on the serving line. Take a good look at all the outfits coming through here. When you see an outfit you think you'd like to be in, you just tell 'em."

I said: "All right, sir." And I went to work on the serving line. I watched troops and watched troops and watched troops! Some were nice; some were unpleasant; some fussed about the food. Finally, a bunch of fellows came in there who walked as straight as a stick; their boots were shined; every button of their uniforms shined; their uniforms were in perfect condition, and they were sharp, sharp, sharp! I looked them all over real good.

Finally, I said to myself: "That's the outfit I want to be in!" When I saw the paratrooper wings on them, I didn't know what the emblems meant. When the day was over, I told the mess officer where I wanted to go and he told me where they were in the camp. I went down there, went in the place and found me a bunk. They called those troopers out every morning before daylight. They would do double-time all around the camp the first thing in the morning. I rolled out of bed and went with them. At roll call the officer said, "And who are you? And what are you doing in our outfit?"

"Sir, it's a long story. Just let me go with you and I'll tell you all about it."

He said, "O.K."

Major Swinson, from Wisconsin, came up to me, talked with me, and asked me where I went to "basic." I told him at Ft. McClellan, Alabama.

"We can't use you," he said.

"Sir!" I said, :"I want to go with this outfit."

So he put my name on the list and said, "Fall in."

We began to double-time, and kept it up for about an hour and a half. We came into the bunks and rested about a half hour. Then we got up and went double-time all the way down to the mess hall. We ate breakfast and double-timed all the way back to the barracks. Then about 10 o'clock they called us out, called us to attention, and told us we had been promised we'd get a furlough before we leave this country. Everybody just cheered! We kept training for a few days, and one night they said, "we're shipping out!"

They had re-issued me different uniforms and I, along with everyone else, got my duffle bag packed with boots. That morning they loaded us up, put us on a train, and away it rolled, pulling in at Camp Shanks, New York! Nobody knew why. All the fellows were wondering **why?** All the officers were talking with each other wondering why.

We stayed at Camp Shanks three days—the first troops to ever occupy that camp. One morning at 2:00 o'clock they came in and woke everybody up. "Meet at the supply tent warehouse pronto," they said. We did. We lined up in front of the warehouse and they issued us weapons, ammunition, parachutes—the whole bit. I didn't know, and none of the rest knew what was up. After they had issued us our clothing and everything you could imagine, they gave me a Thompson submachine gun, which I had never seen the likes of before.

Loaded with our gear, they lined us up and marched us between two long rows of armed guards down to the docks and put us on waiting ferries and headed over to big ships. They loaded the entire division on three ships and set sail. I asked several fellows where we were headed. Nobody seemed to know. Finally, I met a boy from North Carolina who said we were going to Casa Blanca, Africa. I volunteered to help him in the kitchen. That was the first time I ever had fillet minion and eggs for breakfast! That's what we ate on that ship.

We sailed, and sailed, and sailed! One day I heard a lot of yellin' an' bawlin' an' carryin' on. I didn't know what it was all about. Finally, I faced an officer and asked him. He said, "We were called in and set up to go and jump in the Casarene Pass."

I had never had a parachute on, and we were to jump in the Casarene Pass. The officer continued: "We just got word that General Patton has broken through. They say the Panzer Division had him surrounded. We were coming over here to jump behind the lines to help General Patton get out." Perhaps a few were foolhardy enough to be disappointed that we were not called upon right then to undertake a very risky jump but most of us were realistic enough to thank God that "taking casualties" was, for now, avoided.

Our ships pulled into Casa Blanca. Not long after I was ashore, Major Swinson came up to me and said, "I'm sorry, Massengale, but you can't go any farther with us. You stay here in the camp."

I said, "Major Swinson, I wanta' go with you so bad I don't know what to do." Then Major Swinson said:

"Well, you don't have the training. If you're not trained for this outfit, you just can't make it."

"I disagree with you, sir. I can take it. I'm a country boy. I plowed a mule for a livin'. I've got good strong legs on me. And I can make it."

Still not convinced, he said: "I'm sorry, Son, we just can't take you."

So I stayed around the camp there in Casa Blanca for weeks. I had several officers come to me wanting to know what I was doin' there, etc. (And incidentally, this being shipped overseas without any orders, and without anybody knowing you means that they didn't pay my sweet little wife for three solid months. For which the United States Army owes her yet! Married just one year, with a three-month old baby girl, and no income!) If you lose your papers (orders) you may not be a lost soul but being a lost body is a second worst thing, so I discovered.

I asked the inquiring C.O. of the camp where the 82nd Airborne was.

"Yes, I know where the 82nd Airborne Division is. Why? Do you belong to that division?

"No, sir. But I want to."

"Do you know anybody in it?"

"Yes, sir!" I said, "I know Major Swinson."

He said, "I'll get Major Swinson and talk to him for you."

"Sir, I would appreciate that," I said.

The next morning a Jeep pulled up and Major Swinson got out. He walked straight over to me and said: "Massengale, if you want to be with us *that bad,* I'll take you and put you in the Glider Division. You don't need to have jump training for that."

I said, "All right, Sir. That's fine with me, Sir."

They were doing field trips at night in those rough mountains near Casa Blanca. They gave me an 81 mm breastplate. I put it on my shoulders and my back. I walked around in those rocky hills for hours and hours, following those tough guys in their practice and training. That continued until they moved us up to Carawan. We stayed in Carawan only a short time. An airbase was there. One battalion of our paratroopers was flown from there over to Sicily to drop in and wipe out the enemy.

There was a woman on short-wave radio who tried to break the morale of the Allied troops and boost that of theirs. We called her "Axis Sally." She was used by our enemies and maybe at times helped us, too! As we jumped into Sicily, she got on the radio and said, "There are 5,000 paratroopers coming out of airplanes and you'd better get gone immediately." Well, it must have scared the daylights out of the Axis troops because we took Sicily without any problem whatsoever.

I remember one of my friends who jumped there. He and I had black, or very dark hair. I saw him three or four days after the jump. He was gray as he could be! His parachute had 108 bullet holes in it! That's one quick way to change hair color I wouldn't advise! I've heard of things like that but that's the only time in my more than 80 years that I've seen it happen.

From Sicily we went into Naples, Italy, and liberated it. I met some fine people in Naples. There they put me in charge of the Officers' Mess. I cooked them

T-bone steaks, with other good things that went along. Naples had no water and no electricity, so our engineers went to work to help get them going again. Near the officers quarters in Naples there were narrow streets/alleys that separated us from the Italian civilians. The houses had little balconies you could walk out on and reach across and shake hands with your friendly, grateful neighbors. Several times I wished I knew a little more Italian! I was always glad to try to communicate with the several who knew some English. Remembering the people of Naples brings warm feelings into my heart even yet.

One fellow who lived across the alley from us was a jeweler, with a wife and two children. They had no bread and very little food to eat. We got a lot of those dry loaves of what we called "hard tack" (like crackers). We had more of them than we needed, so we shared our extras with them. How happy such a little made them! One time the Air Force flew in a bunch of steaks for our men there—more than we could possibly use up, so I got permission to share a few with that family of four. Not long afterward he came with a box of *exquisite* jewelry. "Send home to your wife!" he said.

I took it to my superior officer who helped carefully wrap it to send to my Ruth back in Atlanta, Georgia. I wish I could tell you she really liked it. But she never got it! Human nature changes slowly everywhere—yes?

We in the 82nd Airborne fought in fourteen different countries in many and varied campaigns. In Germany, once we moved in on LST's. These were landing craft that went up to the beach and let down ramps. Either you had to run down the ramps or jump into the water to swim ashore, whatever the situation dictated. Once we put our duffle bags, supplies, etc, on the craft in front of us. I had taken my favorite picture of my Ruth, wrapped it in paper, then wrapped it in a blanket and put it in the middle of my duffle bag with all my stuff packed around it. When we were going up the canal to land, a German bomber came in and scored a hit right on my duffle bag in the middle of that LC! Quickly it sank to the bottom. I saw it all happen, before my eyes. Later, on shore, I stood trying to hold back tears as I watched the bubbles keep coming up. An officer walked up and saw what I was feeling.

"Soldier, what's the matter?"

"My wife's picture was on that craft, sir."

Rather jovially, he said, "Man, don't cry! **You** could have been on it!" How right he was! Bringing each other quickly back to face reality in the best possible light was part of the ***Lure of the 82*nd *Airborne*** that has made the memory of it live on in the hearts and minds of us survivors now in our 80's. We're just glad to be alive, especially if the computer in one's cranium still works pretty well. (Let's unite to point this careless generation back to the Creator/Preserver of all things good and beautiful.) Some things *are still worth living for, you know—or even worth dying for.*

Many of us remember going into Anzio. It was in a horseshoe shape. We were told that we would have secret service men there with flashlights—a whole bunch of 'em—showing us the way in. We saw flashlights, so the ships pulled up in there. The 36th Ranger Division and several others, infantrymen, were ahead of us. Our enemy had their submachine guns and 88 mm guns zeroed in on us down on that beach. Apparently they had broken our code and pre-empted our plan by capturing our men with lights. Now, sending their own group with flashlights, led us into a giant death-trap. It was a gruesome slaughter on the beach. We started bringing our dead to the ships and putting them in the coolers. Everywhere there were bodies, bodies! Most of the night the gruesome retrieval went on.

Finally, they called for the 505, one of our Italian paratrooper groups who jumped in behind the German lines, back of the mountains. That jump was decisive and we finally were able to get on the beach.

The next morning when we looked at the beach, it appeared like truck loads of red paint in 55-gallon drums had been dumped all over the sand! It was really that red with the blood of our men shot the night before.

That was before we went into Naples, then through Belgium, on to the Rhine River in Cologne, Germany.

A Dark, Dark Night in 1944

You ask me what I remember as perhaps the darkest night in the Allied offensive in Germany? I will tell you.

It was a cold and snowy winter. We were up against the strong and well manned cement pillboxes of the Siegfreid Line. They had slits in the heavy cement through which to shoot at us, and with the white snow we were easy targets. The snow was knee deep, with many drifts waist deep. We were taking heavy casualties. At one point there were so many that our medics were bringing in stiff bodies and stacking them on trucks like cord wood for transport to the rear.

General Gavin came in to relieve General Ridgeway. At one point I saw General Gavin reach up and pull out a handful of his own hair! That, my friend, is *deep grief* and *frustration*! He confided to the British General, Montgomery, that he wondered if we had bitten off more than we could chew. Our troops were at their lowest point in morale that I can remember. It was the cold and snowy winter of 1944–45. Then came

The Miracle of Hot Coffee and Good Food!

I was appointed as an army cook. They sent us plenty of food—like cans of chili and dried eggs. The trouble was many of our cooks did not know how to prepare the available food to make it appetizing and appealing enough to cause the men to want to eat it. When a soldier feels hungry, he is not a "happy camper." Feeling these depressing circumstances, I did some prayerful thinking. I believe our Heavenly Father heard our many prayers.

I made my way to General Gavin. "Sir," I said, "we all know morale is at a very low point. I believe there is something we cooks can do about it. Sir, if you'll give me a driver and a Jeep with a trailer, I would like to make my way over to the Air Force Depot for some supplies to try to do my bit to lift the morale around here. Some good hot coffee on a cold night like this I think would be a good place to start!"

I thought I saw tears come in the General's eyes as we talked. Then he said, "Private Massengale, you've got whatever you need. Good luck!"

My driver and I took off with the Jeep and trailer through that deep snow. We drove, and drove. Finally, we got over to the Air Force Depot. Man, they had everything! Two new 30-gallon garbage cans, gasoline stoves, coffee, steaks—you name it! We loaded the trailer and Jeep and headed back "home" to our pine thicket. I had the men to dig a deep hole in the snow, put two stoves under each can, pour in the water, and wait. Finally, the water in the big cans began to boil. We added the coffee and let it boil. The aroma of the hot coffee began to float among the pines. We tasted it. Delicious!

The last thing to do was pour a bunch of cold water on top of the coffee grounds that made them all settle to the bottom. Now it was time to send for General Gavin and the officers. They thought it was the best coffee they had ever tasted! One of my close buddies told me he just heard General Gavin and Capitan Snow talking about me. Pretty soon General Gavin came over and said, "Massengale, I understand you're a private."

"Yes, sir, that's right, sir."

"Well, Sergeant Massengale, I want you to know that coffee is truly delicious!" That was all he said. But when we got back to the camp, they issued me my stripes. (That meant a raise in pay for me, and a little more in the allotment check for Ruth and little Donna.) Yes, the Lord was good!

Morale began to pick up, and the tide of the war gradually began to turn our way. All the rest is history. I'm confident those on speaking terms with God sent up some "Thank You's" on both sides of the Atlantic. When we crossed the Rhine River, we saw a big wide road, like an expressway. When we saw long lines of German troops walking down that broad road with their hands behind their heads, we began to feel that the war was almost over. They began to load their guns onto our Jeeps, trailers, trucks and any available vehicles. What a mess of guns! I never dreamed of seeing that many guns in my whole lifetime. I still have one of those guns they threw on my truck—a German lugar, made in 1937.

We learned the reason the vast crowds of troops were so eager to come west and surrender to **us**. They were *afraid* of the Russians! They believed we might be humane and show a little mercy, but they were not at all sure of humane treatment if they surrendered to Russian soldiers. The whole Panzer division surrendered to us!

We moved on farther toward Berlin and stopped for the night. What we saw happen that night revealed a basis for the soldiers' fear. We stopped at a big, beautiful house with a large barn with horses in it. We had given the Russians some of our vehicles. It was dark and they were out near the big barn trying to repair a vehicle with a problem. We went to sleep only to be awakened a couple hours later by horses neighing and carrying on terribly! I yelled to the men. We got up to see the big barn on fire. The Russian men needed to have light by which to repair their truck! We grabbed our weapons and headed to the barn. I rescued two of the horses, which the Russians seemed to resent. They were going to let the animals burn along with the barn and hay! One of our officers suggested we just shoot the cruel soldiers, but I was able to restrain them. None of us slept very well the rest of the night because we were so mad at the Russian soldiers for such cruelty to the horses and wanton destruction of a beautiful barn. It was probably good that they were gone by daylight! But we now understood why the German army was so eager to surrender to us before the Russians arrived.

Out of the original company that came from Ft. Bragg, North Carolina, there were only three who came back, and one of the three had been burned over a large percent of his body in a gasoline stove accident toward the end of the war. He got sprayed in the face and all over his body with hot gasoline. His name was Pat Patterson, a Catholic boy from Chicago. He was a baker in civilian life and the best one I ever knew. He and I got into the kitchen together and fed the men first-class food prepared as it should be and the morale shot up into the stratosphere. I did the steaks, etc., and Pat did the baking. What joy we had! He was a prince of a young man. We loved each other like brothers. After the accident they took him from one Army hospital to another and I lost track of him. Finally, my C.O. came to me and said, "Massengale, I know how well you and Pat got along. I know you would like to go see him, wouldn't you?" I told him I surely would.

"Well," he said, "I'll give you a Jeep and a driver and you go find him. No matter where you have to go or how long it takes to find him, just go, and don't come back until you find him."

I said, "Captain, I appreciate that very much. You don't know how *much* I appreciate it."

We started out. The first hospital we came to told us, "Yes, we had Pat here but his case was so severe we sent him to . . . hoping they could do a better job than we could. We didn't have the right equipment." I don't know how many "dead ends" we came into and got a similar answer. Eventually, one said, "He is at . . . where we called and discovered they had the proper equipment. You'll find Pat there." And we did!

I walked up to the side of his bed. He was bandaged from head to foot with only about a 3/4-inch opening in the bandages at the mouth to feed him. I looked into his mouth and saw nothing but blisters. I called his name, and when I called his name he tried to move his arm. I got down close to him and said, "Pat, do you hear me?"

He said, "Yes, Bill, I hear you. And I wanta' tell you something."

"What is it, Pat, that you want to tell me?" (Pat was a devout Christian.) I listened closely to hear his soft, strained answer.

He said, "I've seen nothing for a long time but fire! fire! fire! That's all I see *now:* Fire! Fire! Please go back and tell my buddies and yours: *if hell is anything like this, I want to warn them to avoid it at any cost!*"

Then I promised Pat I would do that. I did my best as soon as I got back to camp to warn every one of our buddies who would listen. I've dedicated the rest of my life to encouraging people to avoid hell and prepare for Heaven.

I want you all to know that out of the agony of that terrible experience with my closest friend in the now-famous 82nd Airborne in World War II, there in Germany, God renewed and deepened my faith and renewed my "call" to share the Good News. That call had first come to me when I was a 14-year-old boy. I didn't obey the "call" when I was young. I thought God was making a mistake in wanting me to preach. But since God delivered me from death so many times in W.W. II, I have tried hard to listen to God and obey Him. I try the best I know to speak up for our Lord at every opportunity that He gives me to share it. I never had the chance to get a formal theological education to be a pastor or "preacher" but I have studied the Bible, God's Word, at home. For years I've taught Sunday School classes, preached wherever I was invited, and filled in as pastor on an interim basis when invited by churches without a pastor. Besides that, I have had a chance to give my personal witness of my Christian faith to countless individuals along the trail these many years. Some became "believers" and began to walk with me the joyous path to *eternal riches.* Others have chosen not to believe. Freedom of choice, I believe, is God's most awesome gift/responsibility! I say that because of the simple truth that freedom to choose equals responsibility for that choice! Shake it any way you want and that's the way it still comes out.

Thoughts Turn Toward Home and Peace

As our responsibilities of World War II began to wind down in Germany, my attention turned back to where it was several years before—to Atlanta, Georgia, U.S.A., and my precious family, starting with my dear wife, Ruth, and baby girl Donna, now almost three years old!

The superior officers began informing us of the "point system" put in place for relieving us from duty over there. "Bill, with having a wife and a child back home, you have plenty of points, so git! Go, man, Go! You'll be going by bus, train, plane, ship, and what-ever—but go! And may God, the Lord, be with you!" That word "go" and the word "home" suddenly were really *"loaded words"* to a big bunch of us. All we needed now was some time and patience. The fitful dreams of the "long night" s-l-o-w-l-y took shape.

I have shared with you just a tiny fraction of my personal experiences of the World War II era in the hope that the sharing may help some of you who made promises to God, as I did, to remember and keep them. I have tried hard to faithfully share the Good News of my personal relationship with our Lord Jesus Christ since those darkest days and nights of the war. That has been, and is, my *goal in life*. Yes, our Lord has kept His promise to me. He said: "But seek ye first the kingdom of God and his righteousness; and all these *things* shall be added unto you as well." (St. Matthew 6:33, KJV.)

What things? I believe whatever we really need, in the amount God can trust us. Some of us seek—and get—financial wealth and it ruins us. Others achieve fortune/fame and use it to bless others and honor God. The choice is ours, from beginning to end. What's in the heart of us is crucial.

In St. Matthew 12:34-35 you can get the summary of many pages of Jesus' teaching on it. Dear family and friends, *things is not where it's at* to put it in colloquial terms!

I know. I've "been there, done that." You can believe me or not. That is your choice, too. I "made my first million" by God's kind providence, plus my hard work and honest dealings. Along came a recession in the housing market and economy. I lost it! My "dream castle" of buying the old home place and retiring to my own little beef cattle operation came down with a devastating crash. At the same time, cancer invaded one of my strong shoulders. There went my vibrant bodily health! Then I got a terrible and unusual eye disease that threatened my sight and limited my driving. Still don't drive much, especially at night. But please hear me out. God, in His own providential and kind way, restored me financially. He also granted the measure of physical healing that I needed to enjoy life by seeing my children's children run and play. I know that healing is temporary, as is all life on this planet. But God is saving the best for an eternity with Him in the place we call *Heaven!* And He has promised it all to everyone who will believe/obey/love Him! Check it out in the "Rule Book" we call the Holy Bible! St. John 3:16 is just one of the nearly a whole page. *Eternal!* What a word, and what a concept! My little brain can't do very much with it but I look forward to *future development* with JOY!

I want to thank my dear wife, Ruth, for her faithfulness to me and our "treasure" Donna while I was gone. A multitude of us young men served our country and, I believe, our loving God for crucial years in the early 1940's. Now our whole world is in another kind of war—a "spiritual" warfare with eternal results/consequences . . . !

My Ruth's nephew, the editor-writer responsible for this and other true "stranger than fiction" stories, J. Robert Boggs, Jr., asked me years ago to take the time to sit down with him long enough to give him this story. My apology that it took so long! He and his wife stopped at our house for two days on the way home from Florida in the spring of 2002. We finally took the time to do what I perhaps should have done sooner. But now it's done, you've read it, and "the ball is in your court." May I ask, how do you intend to make the best use of your awesome "freedom of choice"?

So *gratefully!* "Bill" Massengale

For a big bunch of my buddies who did not get to come back home with us.

2

Rumblings of the Thunderbird

The 45th Division, U.S. Army, 1944–1945

—Francis M. Trotter

MY DRAFT NUMBER, 1001, came up in the fall of 1943. I left Elkhart, Indiana, on January 19, 1944, and was inducted into the U.S. Army on February 9, 1944, at Camp Blanding, Florida. Fifteen or 20 of us were from Elkhart. We spent 17 weeks in basic there, with training in rifle, machine gun and anti-tank guns. I qualified as "expert" in all of them. We would hike up to 25 miles. As company medic, I took care of stragglers with sore feet.

We learned hand-to-hand combat, grenade throwing, and rifle/bayonets so we would know how to handle ourselves in combat.

To help support my wife and two children back in Elkhart, I washed clothes after hours for other guys willing to pay for it. It was $2.00 for fatigues, $1.00 for underwear, and 50 cents for socks. I washed in the shower stalls on the cement floor with GI soap and a brush. I hung them on lines by the barracks. It was up to them to get their own things off the lines.

I also cut hair after hours and on free time on Saturday and Sunday. I charged 35 cents. For more than half the 180 men in the company, I was barber and laundryman. (Strange, what love will enable you to do!) I was also their banker. I kept $100 cash in a cigar box in my footlocker (I left unlocked). We operated on the honor system. They got the money out and put down their names on the notebook. I never had a problem. I told them if anyone ever took any money without writing their name down, they would get clobbered. I sent Ruth and the children $150 to $200 a month, in addition to my Army pay.

When finished with basic, we had a "delay en route" furlough before reporting to Camp Patrick Henry, Virginia. The ten days helped us get insurance and lay plans for any contingency.

The ten days at the Virginia camp was full of letter writing, etc. I even went out for boxing. I boxed a couple of guys in an event promoted by a man who was once Jack Sharkey's trainer. I even boxed him (the trainer) a couple times. In the second fight, I knocked him down. He said, "Next time, I'll get you for that." I said, "No, you won't. I quit. When you get mad, the fun is gone. I quit." That's the way I think of all sports. Keep it fun or just forget it. Don't take sports or yourself too seriously.

One night we had just gone to bed and about 10:00 o'clock they woke us up. "Get up! We're boarding! Get ready to go." We quickly packed our duffle bags and lined up for roll call. They checked us off one by one as we walked up the ramp onto the ship.

The navy men who were handling the boarding told us where to find our quarters on the ship. They filled up the holds first, and then worked their way to the top. There were about four thousand men on the ship. It took four or five hours for everyone to get on board and get situated. About 3:00 a.m., we were all in place and the ship was underway.

When we left port we were met by a naval escort of destroyers that accompanied us to our destination to protect us from submarines. We didn't see any but they told us they were out there. Once when I was on top, I did see two torpedoes and their white wakes. They went across in front of our ship but hit nothing! Our navy escorts then went into action and dropped a lot of depth charges in an effort to sink the submarine. That was near the U.S. coast and it was the only submarine activity we saw.

We G.I.'s didn't know where we were headed but the ship went along the northern coast of South America, then headed across the Atlantic toward Africa. Besides the troop ships, our convoy had oil tankers, supply ships, and the very important navy escort. It was one of the largest convoys in some time. When we left the U.S., we didn't know whether we were headed for the South Pacific or Europe. Now, even though we were zigzagging to avoid submarines, we could tell our general direction was east with Europe as our destination.

I did not sleep in my bunk once during the Atlantic crossing. I slept in a life raft on deck. I didn't want to be in the hold if we were torpedoed! I loved life and felt a responsibility for Ruth and our little son and daughter. Therefore, I took precautions wherever I went. The crossing was fairly smooth with good weather all the way.

Finally, we headed north, up along the west coast of Africa, toward the Straits of Gibraltar. We had a submarine alert again. At this time, the British navy sent escorts down to meet us, and the U.S. escorts turned back. Our new escorts encountered German subs again. (One escort had been sunk on the way to meet us.) I suspect that those who had their "spiritual antenna" up sensed that we were surrounded not only by the British destroyer escort but by God's "guardian angels!" What a comfort! When we were past Gibraltar we had no more encounters with submarines.

We were headed for Naples, Italy, though we fellows still didn't know it. We finally arrived at Naples, disembarked, and went to a staging area. This is where they sent all of us. They must know who/ where you are, to be able to send replacements to the various divisions where they had casualties. Most of us ended up as infantry replacements.

Happily, while I was in the Naples staging area, my brother, Walt, stationed with the U.S. Air Force at Caserta, Italy, learned I was there and came for a three-day visit! We went down to Pompeii and Rome. It was so good to see my brother so far from "home in Indiana!"

Of the men at our staging area, about one thousand of us were sent as replacements for the 45th Division of the 7th Army. Others were assigned to the 3rd Division and the 36th Division.

The 45th Division was called the *Thunderbird Division*. It originally was headquartered in Oklahoma and was made up of National Guard units from Oklahoma, Colorado, Arizona, and New Mexico.

From Naples, my group was transported by a British ship to Marseilles, France. At the Marseilles harbor so many ships had been bombed in the harbor that it was impossible to move our ship to the docks, so we went ashore on LST craft.

With our duffle bags and other equipment ashore, we marched to a quartermaster warehouse where we turned in our duffle bags. The staff emptied the duffle bags, stacked all clothes (and shoes!) by sizes, and kept them in reserve at the warehouse for those who needed them. From then on, all we had were the clothes and jackets we wore, with no "extras." What a change to have no change of clothes!

We were assigned officially to a division company. Mine was to "A" Company, 180th Infantry Regiment of the 45th Division. About two days later, we had our first taste of combat. As we moved forward to take the villages and towns ahead of us, we kept catching up with the Germans who would retreat, but not without a battle. We started fighting for every hedgerow and village. We had more firepower but the Germans fought very hard.

In combat we rotated our companies. "A" Company would attack for one whole day. The next day, "B" Company would take over and "A" would go to the rear to cover the flanks. Next day, "C" Company would lead the attack. Then "A" would again go into the front line. The whole battalion rotated companies in like manner.

Our heavy artillery kept coming up behind us, lobbing shells over us into enemy troops as they retreated. Each company also had a large tank to go along with them for added firepower. If we ran across an enemy tank, it was up to our tank to knock it out.

We seldom attacked in broad daylight, but usually between 2:00 a.m. and 3:00 a.m., which surprised the stubborn enemy. I remember some Mexicans in our division who would climb on top of a German tank, throw a grenade down the hatch and blow it up.

At this time I carried a .45 automatic, my rifle slung over my back, and a Thompson submachine gun in my hands. I also had about six grenades in a strap across my shoulder. Around my waist my ammunition belt had clips for all three of my guns. (Most men didn't carry all three guns.) The reason I carried the submachine gun was that the scout who went ahead of our company was killed. I heard the shot that got him. When I got to him he was dead, so I picked up his submachine gun and ammunition.

I was promoted to sergeant within a week after starting in combat, and was made squad leader. I had 22 men for whom I was responsible. In combat I had to make sure the men were spread out. Bunched up we would make an easy target. But this meant that I was often exposed to enemy fire as I moved about to position the men.

Eventually, in the middle of France, I was promoted to platoon sergeant in charge of the 4th Platoon, about 60 men. The 4th Platoon had machine guns and 20 mm mortars.

Our casualties were pretty heavy in the whole division. In Company "A" we were whittled down from 160 men to about 40 because of deaths and injuries from shrapnel, bullets, grenades, mortar and artillery shells. Our division stopped in Blainesville, France, to wait for replacements for the various units. We were there about a week, reinforced, and pushed on.

We learned to be wary of buildings where snipers might be hiding. One day I asked a farmer standing by the entrance of his old stone house if there were any Germans around. He spoke only a little broken English, but told me there were none in the house. You never knew when to believe them because they would be afraid to tell you if they were there! Standing next to the man, his son, about 9, kept looking at me, then at the barn. I pointed toward the barn, and the boy nodded.

Taking a couple men with me, we went to the barn, called for the Germans to come out, but there was no sound. Then we threw a couple hand grenades into the haymow. Presently, two Germans yelled and came out with their hands up!

As they were being taken away as prisoners, I walked by a manure pile and thought I'd check it out. With a board I pushed some away, and saw the edge of a wooden case. We found two or three cases of concussion hand grenades! I told the farmer and family to get into the house and away from the windows. I took my men around the corner of the house and one shot from my rifle made a tremendous **explosion!** Now, no manure pile, hand grenades or Germans in sight; only the farmer and family laughing with relief that one more real crisis for them had passed!

Towns often harbored snipers. In one small French town we had sniper fire from a building. I took a few men, ran along the side of a nearby building, and entered the building from which the fire had come. Carefully we went from room to room, but nothing. Finally, we got to the third floor with only the attic left to search. We saw the closed lid to the attic, and three of us got in position to throw grenades in different directions through the hole when we opened it. BOOM! and all was quiet. Then we climbed the ladder and found the sniper dead, with his rifle lying by him. I then noticed a gun in the narrow space where the roof met the floor. I crawled back and got the Walther automatic 7.9 mm pistol, which I kept to remember that occasion.

Night patrols were very dangerous. It was on one of these that I believe came closest to death. We were moving through a vineyard in France around 3:00 a.m. It was so dark you could see only five or six feet ahead. We knew the enemy was around, but didn't realize we had come right up to the edge of a machine gun nest. We learned that when Germans ready a machine gun for firing they rack the bolt back in the gun. It makes a slight click. I heard that click right in front of me in the darkness *and hit the dirt.* So did all the men in my platoon. Immediately their machine guns started firing right over our heads! Finally, another one of our platoons figured out what was going on; threw grenades on the machine gunners and wiped them out.

In northern France we met heavy enemy resistance at the Maginot line, with it's reinforced concrete pillboxes. (William Mercer Massengale, of the famed 82nd Airborne Division, has told about this place and occasion also in this book. It was long thought that the Maginot and Siegfried Lines were both impenetrable. But all Hitler had to do when he was ready was, *with lightning speed, go around them!*)

We blasted our way through there at night by dropping Bangalore torpedoes down the vent holes in the fortifications. Bangalore torpedoes were dynamite charges about 3 feet long and 2" in diameter, with a fuse. When the fuse began to burn, like a firecacker fuse, we dropped it down the vent, ran like mad, and waited for the explosion, which came shortly.

When we got to the Siegfried line, it was the same deal. We had to blast them, too. The Germans never thought we'd get through, but we went through in one night's time. From then on, we had to more or less fight the enemy all the way across Germany because they didn't want to give up an inch of the "Fatherland." Again, the casualties on both sides ran very high, but they were higher on the German side because of our superior firepower.

1944–1945—A Hard Cold Winter!

As winter set in, it was very cold. Add to that a foot or two of snow at times, and it can be miserable to be outside, especially when you're out in it 24 hours a day! I agree with Bill Massengale: it was probably the most difficult time to keep up the morale of our troops during W.W. II. Just as optimism and joy are catching, so is gloom; especially when the skies are overcast. Add to that the high casualties that resulted when we began to fight on German soil, and you need help from the Lord who made the skies!

Well, one of these gray, cold days we had pulled up over the crest of a hill and were trying to decide just where we should establish our front for the night. I was walking around talking with the men in my platoon when a sniper's bullet caught me in the right thigh. The bullet went through my right thigh and ricocheted off my left thigh. The medics took me and another injured man to a receiving hospital at the rear. Here they sorted the wounded according to the extent of their wounds—those who needed immediate surgical attention; those who needed to be sent to England, and those to be patched up and sent back to the front.

Like so many of the other men, I also had frozen feet. They tried to thaw out our feet, and considered amputating my right foot, but it began to slowly improve. They cleaned out the wound in my thigh by wrapping gauze around a rod about the size of the bullet, pouring alcohol on the gauze, and pushing it back and forth through the entire length of the wound. Fortunately, it didn't get infection! I was in the hospital for about three weeks—long enough for the wound to start to heal, and they figured I was able to go back to my unit at the front. So they hauled me back up there by truck and then by a jeep. Fortunately, my unit was just rotating to the rear guard that day. I had lighter duties and responsibilities with my same unit a couple days before returning to combat. In the weeks I was gone a lot of my men had been killed or wounded and replacements brought up. I had to get to know these men and what they could do before assigning them responsibilities.

Winter had set in while we were in northern France. The snow was pretty heavy. As we fought our way through the mountain areas, it was *bitter* cold. In the mountains we got our supplies by mule train—part of the "Red Ball Express" as we called them. We kept pushing on, driving the enemy back 24 hours a day. We never let up on them. It seemed to be a "battle of wills" as we hit them with bombs from the air; artillery from our rear, and men in the front lines.

Finally, when we reached the Rhine River, the Germans had already pulled back across the river. After crossing, they blew up the bridges. Our Navy supplied us with 22-foot boats with outboard motors. We crossed at night, with 20 men in each boat. The enemy sank many of our boats, along with the men, giving it everything they had. With all the weapons and ammo you carried, you sank fast. In our section, 24 boats started over but only 11 or 12 made it across. The boat I was in charge of was clear over on the left flank, and the Good Lord took us across without a scratch!

When we got ashore, the Germans were shooting right at us, and quite a number of our men were hit, but we soon cleaned out their machine-gun nests with hand grenades. After we pushed the enemy back, we tried to form a company of men to keep moving ahead. I called the names of my men in the darkness, and found I had only about 12 of the 20 left. The rest had been killed or wounded. We joined with men of other squads, established a beachhead to push on to take high ground. In the moonlight we saw an enemy squad running toward us on a road. We waited until they were about 20 feet from us, then opened up and shot them all. "War is hell" is quite accurate.

During the night our engineers put down Bailey bridges—floating roads supported by pontoons. In the morning, because we had cleared the enemy from the east side of the Rhine, our American tanks and artillery started rolling across. Ambulances and medics also came across so the dead and wounded could be cared for.

Having a good firm foothold east of the Rhine made our job easier, but we had lost many officers and men, as well as equipment in the crossing. After regrouping with the men we had left, we pushed off, still chasing the enemy. Soon our army was re-organized, re-supplied, and ready for more action. But the Germans had also re-organized, and although retreating, they would fight a while and then retreat; fight a while and then retreat. We never retreated. We just kept pushing and pushing—in constant combat.

I'll never forget one young soldier, Harry Evanoff. He had been wounded in one of our battles and sent to the rear for medical attention. After about a month he was back near the front, talking with me about his hospital experience. I was squatting in a foxhole and he was standing there talking to me. He showed me a tin of candy he had just received in the mail from his Sunday School class back home. He was really pleased that they thought of him. He bent down and offered me a piece of the candy, and I took it. He stood up and was eating a piece of the candy. I heard a loud **CRACK!** He fell to the bottom of the hole with the candy in his lap—shot right between the eyes by an enemy sniper. I was mad enough to kill the sniper at the moment, if I could have. But read on and let me tell you another thing that happened in a couple days.

Next morning, when it was just turning light, Hitler's elite SS Troopers that had been flown in from Norway to halt our advance, **attacked.** We could see the big bunch moving toward us, but I signaled our men to hold their fire. Then, when they were about

50 feet from us, I opened fire with my machine gun. All my men joined in. At this range you can't miss! We kept firing at everything that moved—until there was no return fire. A few survivors got back to their own lines, but not many. We held our position all day, waiting for a counter attack, but it never came.

All that day and about half the following night I heard someone moaning. I knew it was one of the SS Troopers we had hit early that morning. Thirty hours is a long time to hear a man moaning, even at a distance. Finally, I asked my buddy if he wanted to go out with me to find the wounded man. "Sure," he said. Carefully, we went toward the moaning and found a youth, 17 or 18, by a tree. I kicked his rifle away, picked it up, and ejected the bullets.

These SS men had dark blue uniforms lined with rabbit fur for warmth. I asked where he was hurt. In perfect English he said he'd been hit in his left arm. I took my knife and cut away his jacket to see the wound. His bicep muscle was all torn. I saw the bone in his upper arm! I told him I was taking him to our medics. I threw him over my shoulder, picked up my rifle, and started toward our medics' station. My buddy walked backward to cover me with his rifle to keep me from being shot in the back.

At the medics station I got a better look at the young German. Nice looking kid, 18 years old. I asked about his family. Said he had a wife and child. He asked me to get his billfold, then showed me pictures of them and his Dad and Mom. It was then that I realized, "the enemy" we were fighting in this war was just as human as we are, with families and similar interests.

When I returned to my platoon, we estimated there were about 200 dead SS Troopers on the ground around our positions. Then we moved on.

That long in continual combat can't be all remembered. But in each situation you say: "It's either him or me." That's how you survive. I learned that it took about seven seconds for a German to zero a target in on his rifle sights, so I was constantly moving. I always ran in a zigzag pattern. We got pretty good at firing from the hip. Our M-1 rifles used an 8-shot clip. I kept firing at the enemy soldiers as I ran. If I didn't get them with the first shot, I might get them on the second or third. When the clip was empty, it ejected automatically. It took one or two seconds to reload.

A German aimed differently. He would lift his rifle to his shoulder, get me in his sights—then fire. It took seven or 8 seconds. Shooting from the hip I could get him first. We sent out patrols of 15 or 20 men, two or three hours before dawn, led by a non-com officer, to silently move forward, right up to the enemy positions to determine their exact locations. Sometimes we took prisoners. At times we got into close combat, taking high casualties. The point man leading the patrol had the most dangerous spot.

One evening Sergeant Springer took me aside to talk to me. He said, "Trotter, I'm supposed to be point man tonight but I wondered if you would lead for me?" I asked him why he wanted me to do it. He said, "I don't know. I've got kind of a strange feeling about tonight's patrol—like I may not come back." So I agreed to take his place as point man. Later that night our patrol moved out. The other men followed me, single file, spaced about every 10 to 15 feet, with Springer as the last man.

We moved along very quietly, and I came to a spot where a couple of Germans were in a foxhole but not aware that we were close by. I relayed the word not to attack now, but we'd get 'em on the way back. Follow me. We moved slowly ahead into German positions. Then I heard the crack of a rifle—just one shot. I passed the word back asking who got shot. After a time the answer came. Sergeant Springer has been killed. He was a fine soldier and I'll always remember him.

Many in our outfit were Indians and Mexicans from the Oklahoma National Guard. Brave fighters, they were. They didn't know what it was to be scared. I especially remember one of these, though I forgot his name. When I asked for volunteers for patrols, he always volunteered. He was a *BIG* man. He was tall, very muscular, with large, powerful hands. He also moved very quietly. A number of times on patrol he got around behind one of their snipers or machine gunners. He grabbed their neck with one hand, and that was it. No scuffle, no cry or shots to alert anyone we were there. And, in spite of volunteering so often for close combat, he got through the war alive and uninjured!

I don't remember the names of many of our officers because they got shot pretty fast. Though they wore the same uniforms as enlisted men, the Germans learned they had their bars painted on the back of their helmets. Our company was supposed to have a captain and three lieutenants. But after heavy action at one time we had no commissioned officers for three months. We "noncoms" ran the company. We got our orders on the radio and did what we had to do.

The 45th Division was moved from one area of the front to another because we had experience in combat. Sometimes we were used at certain points to spearhead U.S. drives, while at other times they used us to repel the German counter-attacks. After one period of hard combat they pulled us back for rest and a new division from the States took over our positions. We were supposed to move some distance from the front, but our leaders just moved a short distance until he saw how the "green" troops fared. The Germans somehow learned of the change in troops and attacked in force. Our inexperienced troops were overrun. It was a massacre. So our 45th Division quickly moved back up, fought hard, and drove the Germans back, but we lost a lot of our men. Many "special" jobs we were assigned because of our experience in hard hand-too-hand combat.

I remember when our objective was Cologne, Germany, a very large city, Our headquarters called for the bombers to blast Cologne. We watched from a mountainside not far away as the B-17s and B-24s dropped bombs all over the city for over an hour. Result? The whole city was ablaze, like a big bonfire, with fires reaching as high as three miles above the city. You would not think anyone could be alive in the city after that bombing. We waited several days for things to cool down before we went in. When we finally went in the people were crawling out of their cellars and basements amid all the rubble, and there was no resistance and no German army in sight.

Then we headed toward Worms. It was the same thing there. The city was blasted, we moved in; no resistance.

Through all the combat, mail kept coming to headquarters for us, but it was hard to get at it. We each had to go get our own. If the enemy saw you moving about through their binoculars, they would lob an artillery shell on you. We had to wait until dusk, when we tried to drop back for chow, and pick up our mail then. Ruth wrote every second day, and Mother about twice a month. Sometimes when days went by between getting back to get it, there were four or five letters. It was always good to get mail so we could keep abreast of what was going on back home.

As we moved forward beyond Cologne and Worms, our infantrymen were spaced about six to 8 feet apart from side to side, and about 25 men deep as they walked and ran ahead. We moved mostly at night and in early morning. In the moonlight it looked like a giant *wave of men, tanks, and artillery* moving across the land. We had to constantly think of land mines. We tried as much as possible to step in the track of the man ahead of us. I was fortunate—I never stepped on a mine. At times you could hear explosions in all directions, which reminded you that your guys were being killed/injured. But there was nothing you could do about it—you just had to keep going.

At night our engineers set up large searchlights behind our lines, spaced about every 500 yards, facing the enemy. These lights showed our men the space for their unit (always *between* the beams and not *in* the light). The strong light partly blinded the enemy, making it difficult to target us.

After Worms, we pushed on toward Nuremburg. In open countryside they shelled us with artillery. I don't know how many men we lost, but lots. I was fortunate to only get a shrapnel would in the lower left leg as I ran in an open field. It felt like someone grabbed me, twisted my leg, and threw me down. I got up, checked myself over, and then saw this piece of shrapnel sticking out of my leg. A medic came and patched it up so I wouldn't lose so much blood. They put me in a jeep and took me to the rear—to a temporary aid station they set up, thence others and me by ambulance to an air base, loaded us on a C-47 twin-engine transport plane and flew us to Paris.

We had no doctor on the plane. Just strapped us in bunks so we would not fall out. We had an exciting landing in Paris. The right engine caught fire. They got us out as soon as the plane landed while they tried to put out the stubborn fire. The fire spread to the whole plane, consuming it there! We thanked God we were out of it!

From the airport they took us to the 48th General Hospital right in the middle of Paris. The U.S. Army had taken over a French hospital to handle all the wounded American soldiers. Many of our GIs never made it to this hospital—they died in hospitals in the rear battle areas—some from wounds; others from shock and loss of blood. There were so many wounded that our doctors and nurses couldn't take care of them fast enough to save them.

I was awarded the Purple Heart the first time I was wounded. Again, an officer came to my bedside and said something to the effect that the U.S. Government was proud to have me as a soldier who was willing to face the enemy and risk my life. . . . A simple, but meaningful ceremony.

In the field hospital where I was first sent, a soldier from an artillery company that had been blown up was shell-shocked. It was his first time to be in action, especially that drastic. He was yelling and screaming! Nurses couldn't quiet him at all. They strapped him to a cot, but he kept yelling. I stood it as long as I could and finally hobbled over to his cot, grabbed him by the collar and told him to **shut up!** I pushed him down on the cot so he would know I meant business. I told him not to think he was the only fellow in the army who ever came under enemy fire. Well, that did the trick! He quieted down and didn't cause any more trouble. "Tough love" they call that? It worked!

At the 48th Hospital in Paris they cleaned my leg wounds and patched me up. In about a week they told me I should get up and walk around so the muscles would heal properly. After the second week I was able to get a pass, go out onto the Paris streets and look around. "Just be back by 10:00 p.m." I always made it my business to get acquainted with the kitchen crew, so I loaded up with oranges and candy bars every day and headed for the city parks. I looked for those who might need it, and shared—like mothers with babies and children. Some of the mothers told me this was the first fruit they had since the war began in 1940! Some would even break off a little piece of the orange and give it to a pretty small baby! What a joy to share a little! It works both ways. I wanted a picture to send home to Ruth. I found a Paris photographer who took my picture. The next day I went to get the picture and he took no money for it! He paid the postage and sent the picture. I gave him a few candy bars and oranges. He practically tore an orange apart to get to the eating of it. Said he had not had one for five years.

I got acquainted with a soldier from Chicago, William Lawry, and we decided to ride the Metro all over and learn as much about Paris as we could. The Eiffel Tower was interesting. Everything was admission free for GI's. We even found an amusement park! We took in the rides and everything! The singing of the birds in the parks reminded us of "back home."

When we'd been in Paris about a month, one day in early May we were on the Champs-Elysses. We suddenly saw people come running out of buildings, and crowds began to mass in the streets! They were shouting, "Fini la guerre!" They were hugging, kissing, screaming and yelling! So we knew the war was over! It was early May of 1945. One guy got down on his knees and hugged me around the legs. People came running up and kissed us GI's on the cheeks. (both cheeks!).

From the hospital I was sent back to my outfit, the 45th Division. It was by truck, a couple hundred miles, I learned that two days after I was wounded, General Headquarters pulled our division off the front lines. I guess they figured the 45th had fought enough battles, so they would let us rest while the 7th Army finished the job. Not long after the 45th was pulled back, the Germans realized their cause was hopeless, so they surrendered. We took two truckloads of noncoms and officers to Nuremburg to see the place where German and Allied leaders met to sign the papers to end the war.

After that we were sent all the way back to Dachau, Germany! We had been there before, and liberated the people from the death camps. We had seen the ovens where they burned the prisoners, and the gas chambers. We were stationed at Dachau *after* the war. Several of us bunked at the house of a Mrs. Hegenmuller for several months. We began training for combat again, because Allied leaders thought we might have to go to Japan to finish the job there. Then in August of 1945 we learned that the atom bombs had been dropped and Japan surrendered.

Then we all thought about going home and getting out of the army.

When the war was over in Germany we drove whatever was moveable of our equipment to Rheims, France, and turned it over to the French government.

From there we went to Le Havre, France, where we boarded ship for Southampton, England. We stayed there a week because they said the New York City harbor could not accommodate our whole Division at one time. With a 3-day pass we were able to see several things in London. One day we hired a taxi to take us to see London. The areas bombed by the German V-1 and V-2 were really devastated—just blown to bits! On the last day I went to 10 Downing Street to see if I could see Mr. Churchill, but he was gone someplace. I also wanted to see if I could locate any of my relatives in England, but that didn't work out either, so we headed back to camp to get ready to board ship for home. We boarded the *Aquitania,* a large ocean liner 902 feet long. It held 11,000 of us! It took five days to cross. The second day we met a severe storm, which lasted three days. They allowed us to go to the second bridge to watch the storm through the windows if we wanted. Many of the men got seasick and didn't care to go, but I wasn't sick, so I went. I was amazed to see the big ship cut through giant waves that would wash over everything. The fifth day the storm quieted and we sailed into N.Y. Harbor before noon. All the harbor boats blew their whistles and shot water into the air. We heard the bells ringing and horns honking all over New York City.

We went to an army camp in New Jersey first. We were quartered there, where we were divided up. Those who had enough points to get out of the army went to their home states to be discharged. I went by train to Fort Benjamin Harrison, in Indiana. It was in September, 1945.

Ruth didn't know I was back in the States until I called and told her I was in Indianapolis! I took a bus to South Bend, and another one from there to Elkhart. I called a cab that took me home to 1623 Morton Avenue. Ruth looked out and saw me coming up the walk. What a joyous return!

It was so wonderful to see Ruth, Scott and Rosemary—even while I had real *pain* in my heart for the families that could never welcome back those they sent.

I was a stranger to our little Rosemary for two or three days. She would run and hide from me. But before long she was over it and accepted me, as our family tried to pick up where we had left off.

October, 1945—Back Home in Indiana!

These recollections are being written in April of 1996. Since the war I have attended reunions of the 45th Division in Oklahoma. Ours was the famous *Thunderbird Division,* and I proudly joined them as a lifetime member of the Oklahoma National Guard.

These memories of combat situations we have written, are not to glorify war in any way. These painful things we have recalled to remind each of us of the cost of freedom. And to help us remember the sacrifices so many—whose names we will never know—made to preserve your freedoms and mine. May we all make an effort to appreciate and keep what came to us at such a cost! We can lose our freedoms! It almost happened to all of Europe in my lifetime. Sad to say, it has happened to most of the world from time to time. Those of us who do not value our freedoms (and the many other Christian values) *enough* to make a determined effort to keep them will most assuredly lose them!

3

God's Answer to My Nazi Teacher

—Reimar Schultze

I WAS BORN in Nazi Germany in 1936. Adolph Hitler had been in power only three years. He ordered that every mother who brought a child into the world should receive ten marks a month for that child. When my oldest brother was born the ten marks started arriving in just a few weeks. When my older sister was born we received ten marks for her. When I was born, several months elapsed but no ten marks came. So my mother went to the government office to find out *why* she did not receive a check for me. (The Germans are known to be punctual people.) As she confronted the officer, he pulled out my birth card and on it were stamped three significant words: "Second degree mongrel."

By the time I was born all Germans were divided into three classes: 1. Jew; 2. Aryan (pure German), and 3. a mixture of Jew and Aryan, which made these a first or second degree mongrel, depending on how many Jewish grandparents you had. My mother was half Jewish and my father was pure German. Mother's parents were from Berlin, and my father was born in Hamburg, Germany.

At that time we lived in Hamburg. The officer who pulled my birth card opened up with a barrage of insults on my dear mother, calling her all sorts of foul things. He called her a "dirty Jew" and berated her for bringing into the world another "little dirty Jew," etc.

After this tongue lashing my mother went home and made a notation in her good old Lutheran German Bible. It was at Psalm 91:11, writing my name and the date in the margin. In English, it says: "For He shall give His angels charge over thee, to keep thee in all thy ways." To "keep" means "protect" in German. My mother had a very quiet, deep faith—so private that she never read to us from the Bible except at times like for the Nativity story at Christmas. She never talked about God to us. She did not tell us about Jesus, or take us to church. It was about this time that the Nazi government forbade Jewish Christians and "mongrels" to attend church or receive baptism and the other rites and privileges offered by the state church. I never knew until I was a young man about my mother's strong, personal faith in God. Actually, it was only after she died at 90 years of age that I discovered from her Bible and other records how much she did read her Bible and write down dates and events that took place.

The next encounter we had with the Nazi party was when they wanted my father to join the party. They told him, "We want you to be a member of the Nazi party, but to join you must divorce yourself from your Jewish wife and disown your children!"

His response: "I love my wife and my children, and I'll never leave them." The next day when he went to work he discovered he was fired from his job. The harassment continued, and got worse in Hamburg. Also, it was about this time that Hamburg began to be bombed by the British. Every night we would have to leave our 5th floor apartment and take the stairs all the way to the basement because of the bombing raids. Most nights we had to head down to the basement two or three times. All this time his Nazi party "friends?" kept hounding him to divorce his Jewish wife and children. He finally sensed that he had to do something drastic, so he took his family and moved to a small town far over into East Germany. A few months after we had left the city of Hamburg, the whole block where we had lived there was leveled by British bombs. That night was called "the night of fire." More than 50,000 civilians were killed in one night! Only four survived in that whole block! In this case the severe persecution worked to keep us safe. "He shall give His angels charge over thee to keep thee in all thy ways."

In our little town in East Germany, my father found a job some distance away. It took him an hour each way to work. I can't remember seeing him more than a couple times when I was a child. We were usually in bed when he got home and were still in bed when he left for work. He literally worked himself to death. Long hours and hard work took their toll and he died at age 39.

At this time the Soviet army came near, moving toward Berlin. Our town was filled with refugees and bumper to bumper traffic. The horses the soldiers rode were so poor, some looked almost like skeletons in that cold winter. The old men and women on some of the wagons were freezing and dying. My older brother went to school one day and saw the bodies of about 1,000 German soldiers stacked on the big school lot, frozen—piled like cordwood. There was no time for burial. At this same time Jews were being killed right there in our little city. My mother had no idea just when the Nazi officials might knock on our door to take us all away to be exterminated.

As if this were not difficulties enough, my mother gave birth to her fifth child some months after our father had died. I was nine years old as death by star-vation came knocking on doors in that city, with the Red army approaching from the east. The city was not a good place at a time like this, so our mother tried every way she knew to get out. Truckloads of people, like frightened animals being hauled to mar-ket, were turned back time and again. There was no place to go!

I remember hearing on the radio that the German army would try to evacuate a train load of seriously wounded SS troops from our city and leave the city for the Red Army to pillage. They said there would be some standing room on the train for a limited num-ber of refugees. Since the one train had limited space, the qualifications for boarding were: There must be at least three children who had to be orphans or half orphans, plus one child had to be an infant. Wow! My father had to die and the fifth child had to be born to qualify our family to get on the train. I clearly recall my mother gathering up four children around her as she held the baby. "Children, shall we go or stay?" I remember the four of us said as with **one voice: "Let's get out of here!"**

My mother wrote later in her memoirs: "I took the voices of my children as the voice of God.: We took the train, with the agony involved."

In a matter of minutes, without going to the bank, our 39-year-old mother wrapped the baby in a blan-ket, loaded us four children with whatever we could carry, and we waded through snow almost knee-deep headed for the railroad station. We were *eager* to escape from the Communist Red Army.

At the depot we stood in the snow and waited that night for hours as the wounded soldiers were loaded on the train. There was no place to sit. In the boxcars there were four rows of hospital beds, stacked four levels high. Between these beds there were these little spaces where we refugees could stand. It was supposed to take two hours to travel to the city of Danzig. But it took us three days and three nights to get there, all the while the SS soldiers were groaning and dying all around us. No food; no medicine; no heat; no rest rooms. The German city, Danzig, is now the Polish city of Gadansk.

Why did a two-hour journey take three days and nights? Because at times the Red army got ahead of us and damaged the tracks, and our troops would drive them back and fix the track as best they could so that the train could slowly get past. We heard artillery fire off and on all that time.

My mother said that so far as she could tell, all the wounded men on the train were abandoned to die when we arrived at Danzig. The verses of Psalm 91 my mother underlined shortly after I was born nine years earlier spoke *truth.*

Remember that, according to my birth card when I was born in Hamburg, Germany, I was classified as a second-degree mongrel. That was because my mother was half Jewish. Shortly before the British bombs leveled the section of Hamburg where we lived, my father took his wife and family to a town in East Germany. There he got a job, worked long hours, and died young at age 39. Later, just 24 hours before the Red army rolled into our city from the east, my mother escaped with her five children via a German troop train to Danzig. There thousands of us were locked in between the Soviet forces and our backs toward the Baltic Sea. The only way out was by ship through the Baltic Sea. Hitler ordered the largest refugee evacuation in history from this area. But the Russian submarines and torpedo boats were sinking many ships. Twenty-two thousand refugees went to cold watery graves in the Baltic Sea. My brother and I heard of one last refugee ship yet taking out refugees, so my mother took us and got on it. The fog was so thick you could not see the front of the ship from the back of it. Men with long poles helped to fend off the mines in the waters outside the harbor.

Remember the place my mother wrote my name in her German Bible was Psalm 91:11: *For he will command His angels concerning you to guard you in all your ways; they will lift you up in their hands, so that you will not strike your foot against a stone.* (NIV).

Since the German harbors were mined, our ship went to Copenhagen, Denmark, where we were unloaded and taken to a refugee camp. Two years we lived behind barbed wire (36,000 of us) with 17 people in our room. My baby sister, with many others, died of starvation and was buried in a mass grave. She was born to get her family out of the hands of the Russian Communists. That was her mission.

In our room of 17 people, our family of five had two bunk beds. As I was trying to sleep each night, on that bed of straw, I began to wonder about the meaning of life. After a year at the refugee camp, the people decided to start a school. There were no books or school equipment for a school except a blackboard, a teacher and a piece of chalk, but the refugees decided to have a school consisting of elementary school, high school, and university. One thing we memorized was the great German hymn, "A Mighty Fortress Is Our God. . . . "—my first religious education. On my bunk I meditated on the word "God." Who is God? Where is God? It seems to me that I was a bit like the boy Samuel in the Bible who heard a voice in the night, but could not distinguish who it was that spoke to him.

But thank God, about a year later, as we returned to Hamburg, I had my first personal experience with God. I still remember the day when I had gone out into the forest. I wanted to get away from the city, which was 78% destroyed. Since I had no tent or blanket, I slept under some pine branches. As I awakened in the morning and the golden beams of the sun were coming through the birch trees, I heard a voice speaking to me. The voice said:

"I love you! I love you! I AM LOVE!"

Since there was no one around except me, I knew it had to be God speaking to me. This was the *first* time I ever recognized God's voice when He spoke to me. Then God told me:

All the trouble and all the suffering you see all about you is not of my making. It's there because of man's inhumanity to man.

Now, dear ones, I don't know how you may want to fit this into your theology. But I want you to know that I had no theology, and knew nothing about God or Jesus. Yet, this Creator/Sustainer/Redeeming God spoke to me directly and personally—just one of the millions of the spiritually hungering young people in His beautiful, but fallen world!

Which leads me to an observation: Sometimes people with no theology may experience more of God than those with a lot of theology!

So God told this 13-year-old boy that He loved him! Of course, I knew my mother loved me. I never heard her say "I love you" in words, but she, a young widow, demonstrated it by working so hard to keep all of us, her children, alive during those difficult days.

Let me share another story with you. When I was 16, I was about to graduate from high school. In Germany, we started at 12 and ended at 16. In the last year we were presented with Charles Darwin's evolution theory. Listening to the teacher I could not put things together in my head. Looking around the classroom, I thought, according to Charles Darwin, some of the students should have been, say 10%, ape, or whatever. But in my class of about 500 students, I could not find *any* that, to me, looked like anything but homo sapiens. As I meditated on all this, there was something deep inside me, though I had no word for it, telling me this evolution thing was false. It did not have the "ring" of truth in it.

Then, to close this discussion, the teacher asked: "Is there anyone who wants to try to disprove this theory of evolution?"

Without my wanting to, without planning to or any forethought at all, my 6-foot-four frame stood up and I said: "Tomorrow I must speak against this." I want you to know that I was the most shy, the most introverted boy in this all-boy high school! Nobody had ever heard me say a word in the nearly four years except a shy "hello" or the like. Now, I knew I had to speak before the whole class! Be assured that what got me on my feet was not *my* idea or my will but the power of God!

When I sat down the professor said, "Mr. Schultze, you will have all the science hour tomorrow."

That day when I went home, for the first time in my life, I asked my mother if she had a Bible. She pulled out her old Lutheran Bible and handed it to me. I took it and thought surely I would find something in it that proved Darwin's theory of evolution was wrong. In most books the last chapter is a summary, in one form or another, of what the book is about. Since I wanted to be a medical doctor, I figured the last part, the Revelation, would give me that summary, or conclusion. But the "Revelation" was not a revelation to me. It was utter confusion!

So when I went to bed that night I said: "God, Almighty, whoever you are, tomorrow is *your* hour. You must tell me what to say." Then I went to sleep and rested well. Next day in science class, as I stood up to speak, the silence was deafening. Then, after several seconds—that seemed to me like hours—these words came out of my mouth: "It cannot be! It cannot be! There must be a God! There *must* be a God!" These were the only words that came from my lips and, after waiting a few moments for more words that did not come, I made my way back to my seat against the back wall of the classroom. Just as I was ready to slide into my seat, the glory of God came upon me! And again the "inner voice" of God spoke to me. He said, "I will give you the answers to the questions as to origins, purpose and destiny."

You see, just a few weeks before that, I had been saying to myself. What am I here for? Where did I come from? And where will I go when I die?" I had been wrestling with *the* **biggest questions of life.** The world's educational systems do not answer those most basic questions of life, and here God speaks to this 16-year-old and promises to give him the answers to life's most important questions! I was excited and thrilled more than I can possibly tell you. Now, from that day on, the biggest thing I had on my mind or entertained as a purpose in my heart was to know God. After school I ran, walked, and ran some more to get home as quickly as I could to read the Bible and pray to this "unknown" God. My thirst seemed unquenchable and my desire to really know this God and His truth took me down town to a minister of the state church. I said: Sir, I'd like to know what to do to make it to Heaven. What can I do to make sure that I'm pleasing God and will make it to Heaven when I die?'

He said to me, "Young man, just be sure you do more good things than you do bad things and you'll make it to Heaven." I began to wonder just how I would ever know if I did more good deeds than bad deeds! So I returned home confused and disappointed but still determined to pray to the "unknown God" every day and to read the Bible.

After two months more of reading the Bible, I finally found two passages that made sense to me. One was the words of Jesus in Matthew 7:7, "Ask and it will be given you; seek and you will find; knock and the door will be opened to you."

I said, "God, if there was ever a German boy who was asking, seeking and knocking, it is I. And if You don't open the door of truth; if You don't answer my prayers, then the Bible is not for real, and it's all a big farce."

The other scripture I found was, of all places, in the Revelation 3:20, *Behold, I stand at the door and knock; if any man hears my voice and opens the door, I will come in to him and will live with him, and he with me.* I saw clearly that Jesus wanted to come into the heart of me, but I really didn't know how to make this happen.

Then, six months after God had me challenge Darwin's theory of evolution in high school, I received an invitation to visit my Jewish grandfather in England. (He was smuggled out of Germany during the Holocaust by a German church that had a special love for the Jewish people.) It was while I was visiting my Jewish grandparents in England, on the last day I was there I received a personal invitation via a post card from an English evangelist by the name of Major Ian Thomas. He had a Bible conference there in northern England. Somehow, he had heard about my being in England and he invited me to come up for a few days.

I was full of adventure and I was seeking after God, so I wrote a post card back to my German teacher to explain. I said: "Dear Sir: I'm sorry I will return late for school this year. In compensation for being late I will offer to give a speech in the English language. Signed, Reimar Schultze."

I arrived at Major Ian Thomas' Conference Center, which was an old English castle. Young people from all over Europe met there in a lovely ball room for tea. I felt the presence of God there in that room as I did in the forest in Germany when God spoke to me the first time. So, I asked several of the German boys what I must do to be "saved." They tried to lead me to the Lord Jesus, but they didn't know how. They finally said: "Major Ian Thomas is in his office right now. Why don't we take you to his office, and maybe he will be able to help you."

So I went to Major Thomas' comfortable office (as only the English know how to make an office comfortable!) He told me about Jesus, how He came from Heaven, how He shed his blood for me and died; how He took the punishment of my sin upon Himself, that I might have everlasting life. He said that I must *believe* in Him, invite Him into my heart, and then serve Him the rest of my life. Then he said: "In light of all this that Jesus has done for you, may I ask you another question: Do you sense that Christ is knocking at the door of your heart?"

And I said, "I surely do!"

Then Major Thomas asked: "Are you willing to let Him come in?"

I said: "I surely will."

Then he took me to Romans 10:9. It says "that if you confess with your mouth that Jesus is Lord, and believe in your heart that God has raised Him from the dead, you shall be saved." He asked me if it said maybe or perhaps, and I said, "No! It says shall be saved." So I anchored my faith to that firm foundation rock and it worked! That was about 50 years ago that it started working in me and for me, and it is still working! I felt the presence of the Lord Jesus by the Holy Spirit invading my heart, my soul, my whole being. The burden of my sins was lifted off me, and I knew and I felt that I was a "new man" in the Lord Jesus Christ. Then I began to thank the Lord for what He had done. Before I made my way back to the hayloft where I was to sleep, which was over the place the horses were kept, Ian Thomas asked me if I would give my testimony the next morning. The idea scared me! I told Major Thomas that I wanted to leave early the next morning to cross the channel back to home. So I played "Jonah" because I was too afraid to stay and give my testimony at breakfast and I paid a high price for my cowardice. We must all learn obedience by the things we suffer for disobedience! A storm arose early the next morning and the channel crossing was cancelled, making necessary another night in London! My money ran out and for two days I did not eat. When I did cross the channel to Germany, I got terribly seasick. Did you ever have to vomit after fasting two days? You try to get your empty "insides" up and out, but find them still attached somehow. They won't come up!

With water spraying over the ship, I got wet and cold, adding to my misery. If you didn't know it, God may allow the devil to help "spank" us for our disobedience! The "enemy" seems to delight in pouring it on when we are discouraged. Looking into the darkness of the angrily churning English Channel, the devil sarcastically said to me: "Son, how do you like being a Christian now? How do you like being 'saved'?" (This was the first time I was ever aware of meeting the old "devil" face to face.) In response, this 16-year-old German boy replied: "Old 'devil,' even if I go to hell, I'm going to talk of Jesus until you get so sick and tired of me you'll spit me out of that place! I'm serving notice right now that I'm in this for better or worse."

It was there on the stormy British Channel in August of 1952 that I signed my "marriage contract" with God, "for better or for worse." And may I suggest to each of you that you remove the "reverse gear" completely from your relationship with God! I also suggest that you remove the "reverse gear" from your marriage, and never even think of divorce. IF you will take that same positive attitude in all areas of your life, you will have a *positively* successful time in your religious, social, domestic, business, and every other part of your life!

Please forgive us if we Christians have left you with the false notion that if you follow the true Messiah and Lord, Jesus, from then on everything will always be for you a "bed of roses." Jesus didn't say that! Nor does our life experiences say that. Check it out! But the real "pay checks" or rewards for serving the true and living God are infinitely better than the consequence and/or rewards of following Satan. I believe it holds true for this earthly life and for what follows it in eternity. There's nothing like it. Millions of us have seen both sides, having walked in darkness and now are walking in the light of God's truth and in fellowship with His Holy Spirit.

I'm grateful for the privilege of adding my words of testimony in this book my friend, J. Robert Boggs, has put together to tell of God's wonderful mercies and deliverance in the lives of many others from all walks of life. I'm confident my friend of many years would not mind if I tell you that for many years the theme of my life and writing has been the "Call to Obedience." I believe God's Holy Spirit has been sending throughout the world people for whom Christ gave His very life! I challenge you, dear one. to purpose deep in your heart to simply obey God no matter what!

Editorial Comment: My friend of many years, Reimar Schultze migrated to the USA. He pastored a church in Nebraska before going to Kokomo, Indiana, where he's a busy pastor. Among other responsibilities, he produces a radio program that pretty much reaches around the globe. Reimar Schultze is a talented writer whose upcoming book "Abiding in Christ," The Essence of Christianity by CTO Books, P.O. Box 825 Kokomo IN 46903 you will want to read. He and his wife have reared a splendid, talented family. I'm grateful to him for this chapter in my book.

J. Robert Boggs, Jr.

4

Diamonds from the Mines of Manhattan

—R. Anthony Vigna and J. Robert Boggs

In their youth Frank Paul Vigna and Rosa Russo came to New York City from their native Italy. Frank, with his parents in March, 1885. Rosa came with her parents, in December of 1897. Their families settled in an Italian neighborhood in lower Manhattan. Immigration officials put them there to make them feel at home as much as possible in this *big, new* and *strange* land.

Frank and Rosa grew up not far apart in their parents' adopted homeland. It was expected that young people would get the best job they could find and work to help support the family. *Surviving* was a "family affair." Early they learned valuable "togetherness" lessons. *Together* they "sank or swam." Diligence and determination were two big factors that helped most families "survive" with not much to spare.

It was customary in those days for parents of sons to get together with parents who had daughters and "arrange" marriages for their offspring. Frank and Rosa's parents did that, and the two were happily married in St. Anthony's Roman Catholic Church up the street.

As usual children soon began arriving, making hearts glad—and necessitating the adding rooms to

Frank and Rosa's crowded flat! In a few short years they had three small sons and Rosa was with child again.

November 2, 1910, the faithful midwife came to visit. After the examination she said, "Rosa! in just a couple a' days I predict you're gonna' have another fine baby boy!"

When the midwife left, Rosa said to her mother, "Well, Mama, if the baby's a comin' that soon, I better get the house cleaned and the curtains washed." So she started the project.

While Rosa was reaching to put the curtains back up, she had a pain. "Mama! Come and help me. I think the baby's a-comin'!"

Mama came running, and after one glance, took command of the situation: "Run! Find the midwife and bring her back—quick!" While someone was on their way to get her, "Mama" helped get Rosa off the chair and to bed, and when the faithful midwife returned, Rosa and the baby were safely in bed, and *all was well*. They named this fourth son "Anthony" for a famous Italian saint.

It was customary in those days for mothers to stay in bed for a week after the birth of a child. On the eighth day, Rosa's mother said, "It's been a full week since the baby came. Don't you think you better take a walk an' get some fresh air? And put on a sweater! It's November already, an' you don't wanna' catch a cold."

The cool air was invigorating, and seeing the blue sky lifted Rosa's spirit. On her walk down 23rd street she heard beautiful Italian music coming from across the street. The Episcopalian Italian Mission was having midweek service. It sounded *so good* that Rosa just *had* to go over to investigate. Once inside the chapel she could see the happy faces of people singing *with* the organ music. Then she knew why she had been drawn, like a magnet, across the street. A kind lady (a Mrs. Mignona) smiled at Rosa and motioned for her to come and sit with her. She did, and sat entranced for the rest of the service.

Rosa had so much joy in her heart that the distance home seemed very short. Mama, seeing her smiling daughter coming, flung open the door with, "Rosa! Where you been? You had me so worried!! You were gone almost an hour and a half. I was afraid someone had kidnapped you. More than one beautiful woman like you has been grabbed off the streets of New York and. . . ."

"Mama! Mama! Please stop long enough for me to tell you where I've been, all right?" On my nice walk I heard this beautiful music from across the street. The people were singing in Italian, and I went over to investigate. The music was coming from the Italian Episcopal Mission. A nice lady invited me to sit with her, and I did. Oh, Mama! I felt *joy* in that chapel! The lady took my address and said she'd visit me sometime. Now isn't that just wonderful! I can hardly wait to see her again!" Rosa assured her mother that it seemed perfectly safe on the streets of New York that evening, and reminded her that it was not really dark yet.

Hungers of the Heart

Somewhere near this point in the history of these immigrant families, the spiritual nature—*the hungers of the hearts*—of the Vigna and Russo dads and moms began to surface. Grandpa Russo, after some gentle prodding by his good wife, decided it was time he went to church more. One bright Sunday morning he stopped by the Vigna's at 406 E. 24th street, dressed in a suit he hadn't put on for a while.

"Papa, where you goin' all dressed up?" asked his daughter Rosa. "I'm a gonna' go to church," he proudly replied. After affectionate hugs for his grandsons and a little kiss on Rosa's cheek, out he walked and headed down the street toward the St. Anthony's church.

After about 20 minutes—with Frank still in bed (sleeping in after the late card game the night before) and Rosa and the children finishing breakfast—here came back a flustered-looking Grandpa Russo.

"Papa! What's a-matter? You said you was a-goin' to church! Why are you back so soon?" While Grandpa caught his breath, in walked sleepy-eyed Frank Paul just in time to hear Grandpa's answer.

"You won't believe this, but it just happened! When I walked up the church steps, the usher met me with his hand out and says: 'Fifteen-a-cents, please! I felt for my change purse, an' remembered it was in my other pants. So, I told the man that, and promised to give him 30 cents next Sunday. But he said, 'No fifteen-a-cents, no seat.' So, here I am back already. I'm not goin' back. Remember I told you that church just wants money?"

He didn't return; nor did the Vigna family have very strong church ties for some time after that memorable Sunday. But that tragic little episode did *not* end their spiritual hungers. As St. Augustine said centuries ago, "We are made for You, O God, and our hearts are restless until they find rest in You."

Frank Paul Vigna continued to work in the printing business and Rosa continued to bear children and teach them, as best she could, how to survive the "ways of the world" and stay alive in the big city. She also taught them the Christian principles and traditions that had been handed down to her via many generations. She had an eye for the *beautiful* and a heart for what was *proper* and *right*. She allowed no temporary setbacks in life to cause her to give up and forsake her spiritual needs—those *hungers of the heart*.

Let us pick up the story now in the middle of November, 1910. About ten o'clock on a Monday morning there came a knock on Rosa Vigna's door. Through the curtain Rosa sees one of those kind ladies she had met at the mission not long ago. She eagerly opened the door. The lady introduced herself as Gina Grana, from the Episcopal Mission. She said: "Mrs. Mignona, whom you met not long ago sent me to give you my testimony and talk with you about our Lord Jesus."

"Oh, come in! Come in!" said Rosa, as she gave the little lady a welcome, warm hug. "My hopes were *so* high that you or she could come to see me. Now please tell me how to find the joy I saw in you people at the Mission. The happiness you have there must be catching. I've felt it inside me since then, every time I *thought* about that Wednesday night! Come, and let's sit here at the kitchen table."

The lady explained that true *joy* comes when people ask Jesus not only to forgive their sins, but when they sincerely invite the Spirit of Jesus (the Holy Spirit) to come into their hearts to *stay,* or "abide." She said that where Jesus is there is *joy* and *peace*—and real love. "I invited Jesus into my life some years ago. I told Him I was giving my life (surrendering it) to Him, and I asked Him to come into my life and just, 'take over.' Since I sincerely made that commitment to Him, I have had true joy and happiness deep inside me, *no matter how rough the road or how deep the sorrow.*" Rosa could see and *feel* that the lady was speaking pure truth to her eager ears.

"Oh, my dear sister, that is just what I have wanted—have hungered and thirsted for—all my life. And here you have come to tell me more about it! Thank you! Thank you again for coming!"

Gina explained to Rosa that when she was young in Italy she studied to be a nun. Since then she had come to America, married a concert violinist, and now she was doing her best to help others to know Jesus personally as Savior and Lord. At a pause in the dialog, a cloud came over Rosa's face. "Do you have a question?" asked Gina.

"Yes" replied Rosa. "I can tell by the joy on your face that you have what I would like to have. And I'm so happy for you. But you are a very religious person, and I'm not. I'm just—ordinary. I feel sure that I could never have the joy and happiness you have found."

"Oh! But Rosa! That's the true beauty of this *good news! It's for everyone!* Really! God is 'no respecter of persons.' It says so, right in your Bible! Do you have a Bible?"

Rosa went over and reverently handed her their treasured family Bible. Gina opened it to Acts 10:34. "See, it says right here: 'God is no respecter of persons.' That means that God loves everybody! He has no 'pets.' He treats us all alike." Rosa leaned forward, with eager anticipation written on her beautiful, reverent face.

"Now let me show you *more* wonderful verses from God's Book. You and I both know a little bit about Rome, back in Italy. Paul the Apostle wrote a letter to the church there in century one. Look here in Romans 3:23. It says: 'We have all sinned, and come short of the glory of God.' That's why Jesus told Nicodemus that we *must* be born again, or have a spiritual birth, in order to see the kingdom of God. (St. John 3:3)

"And Romans 6:23a reminds us that 'the wages of sin is death.' How can anyone escape the finality of that death sentence? By asking for and receiving God's gift of salvation and *life*—in and through Jesus Christ our Lord. Now, just a few pages over, St. Paul, in three short verses, sums it all up for us: 'That if you confess with your mouth *Jesus is Lord* and believe in your heart that God raised Him from the dead, you will be saved. For it is with your heart that you believe, and are justified; and it is with your mouth that you confess and are saved.' Notice verse 13 that says, 'Everyone who calls on the name of the Lord will be saved.' " (10:9–13).

"Dear Rosa, do you believe God's Word?"

Without hesitation Rosa answered, "Yes, I do believe it!"

"Then follow me in this prayer: 'Lord Jesus, I ask you to forgive all my sins, and save my soul, just like you promised. Come into me and make my heart your permanent dwelling place. Your word says if I call on you, you will save me. I'm calling on you, and I now *thank* You for saving me. Amen!"

Rosa Vigna looked up at her new "sister in Christ," Gina Grana, with a beautiful smile on her face and said, "He did it! Just like He said! Oh! Thank You, Thank You, Lord Jesus!"

That was only the first of a multitude of expressions of Rosa's deep, deep gratitude to her new-found Savior and Lord that would continue for many years to come—really as long as she lived!

Rosa was the first of a BIG handful of *diamonds* from just *one* family; the Vigna's, from the *Mines of Manhattan!* Gina Grana, immigrant from Italy, did the digging, assisted by Mrs. Mignona, and who knows how many others? The polishing, cutting, and setting of these precious jewels God did through Pastors Robert and Marie Brown, of Glad Tidings Hall, down on 42nd St., along with a great crowd of others, many of whose names are known only to God. But they *will* all be remembered! And *rewarded* by the God of all Creation on that *Great Day* that is sure to come some time.

Sharing the Good News!

What's the first thing you want to do when something really good happens"? *Share* the good news, of course! Rosa could hardly wait for her husband, Frank, to come home from work late that night to tell him what had happened to her. He listened with interest, then said: "Rosa dear, that's great for *you*. You deserve it, 'cause you're a *good* woman. But me? I'm a *bad* man. I swear, play cards; I gamble, drink, lie, and do about all the bad stuff you can mention. Religion has never done me much good, I guess. I'm sorta' hopeless. O.K.?"

"Oh, but Frank, the nice lady said *it's for everybody!* And she's coming back and would like to talk to you too!"

Seeing a hurt look come over Rosa's lovely face, Frank finally said, "Well Sweetheart, I've gotta' get to bed. But *if* the good lady *does* come back, tell her I'll go to church *if* she knows one where they speak American. My Italian is already gettin' rusty on me. Good night."

Frank thought he was, "safe" because he didn't expect the lady to come back. Nor did he think there was an English-speaking church anywhere close by there. But the very next week Gina returned, which made Rosa's heart dance with delight. When Rosa asked if she knew of an English-speaking church, she gave Rosa a card with the name and address of the Gospel Hall on 42nd St., with hours of services, which created the desire in Frank to be there on Wednesday night.

Rosa could hardly wait until Frank got home that night. She shared with him the delightful time she had again with Gina, and showed him the address of the English-speaking church. Frank looked at it and exclaimed: "That's less than two blocks from where I work! I think I'll just go there after work tomorrow and stay for the Wednesday evening service. Don't look for me home 'til late."

Rosa put the children to bed and waited up for Frank. When he got home he was so excited he could hardly sleep. "Please tell me about it" Rosa pled.

"Oh, Rosa! It was *so* wonderful! I can't start on it tonight, else I'd not get enough sleep to go to work tomorrow. I'll tell you and the boys *all about it* when I get home from work tomorrow. But I'll tell you this much: I found Jesus, like you did. You were so right! It *is* wonderful."

Rosa was especially eager for Frank to get home from work Thursday night, and Frank could hardly wait to tell her all about the "good news." Her curiosity started that morning when Frank wasn't there to light up his pipe while she was getting his breakfast. In fact, he *and* the pipe were gone! She thought he might be down the hall at the shared bath. She took a key to investigate and he was not there. The mystery of the "missing husband" was solved when she walked back into the kitchen and saw the bottom of his shoes under the edge of the table! He was *under* the table, kneeling and praying! Later, his prayer over the food was haltingly "ad lib," but "from the heart"—and a bit longer than usual too. Talk about "firsts!" They were coming with such speed that it almost made Rosa's head swim. But the changes were not complete surprises. Rosa had been praying for her husband ever since Gina had led her to a vital faith in Jesus.

This "New Man" Talks to His Wife & Boys

Next came the real *feast!* Thursday evening Rosa had prepared the best dinner for Frank and the children she could possibly afford. Young Vincent, James, and Henry seemed to sense that this was a "special" evening. Tony, (the baby) would have been very excited too. Several years later he was given all the vital reports when he was old enough to understand. At eight years of age he received Christ as *his* Savior and was baptized later in water at 14 years of age.

Here's a summary of what was later related to Tony: As soon as Frank was off work on Wednesday, he headed for the address Gina had given Rosa. He found the *Glad Tidings Hall,* and was the first one there. Later a man came to unlock the place and welcome him, saying: "You may have any seat you want." Eventually Pastor Robert Brown came, the people gathered and the lively service started. The praying was quite vocal and the singing was lively, and finally Pastor Brown gave the 'invitation.' His instructions were:

- Raise your hand if you are interested in being 'saved' and want me to pray for you. (Frank's hand went up.)
- If you 'mean business' please stand. (Frank stood.)
- If you *really* mean business with God, please walk down to this altar of prayer. (Frank stepped forward.)

Kneeling there with others, a counselor asked him: "Do you want to be 'saved.'"?

"That's why I'm here" Frank replied rather impatiently.

"Then please follow me in this prayer."

With tears rolling, Frank repeated: *"O God, be merciful to me, a sinner! . . . Cleanse me from all my sins and save me for Jesus' sake. Amen."* It was a brief and simple prayer, but made from a penitent, hungry heart, and Frank knew deep inside him that God had heard and answered it. He later stated: "I felt like someone had taken an old dirty coat from me, and put on me a pure, white robe. As I walked home from 42nd St. at Tenth Ave. down to 24th St. and 1st Ave., *the stars had never seemed so bright and so very beautiful in all my life."*

This, in brief, was Frank's report to Rosa and the boys. Then Frank said, "Boys, your mother and I want to take you with us to the Episcopal Mission up the street to the Thursday night service. I want you to help me pass out some Gospel tracts along the way and invite people to our Lord Jesus. So, let's get ready and go!" And *Go* they did! From that day until he died at 69, Frank never slackened his pace.

From *day one* he was an untiring witness for *Him* who had forgiven him, and had re-made him into the clean vessel He could trust and use in the diverse, needy place called New York City.

From that beautiful November day when Frank Vigna was 42 until he slipped away at age 69 to the *Heavenly City,* God used him to find a *multitude* of souls. His labor, giving, and work in his own church was untiring. But he did not stop there. His passion for sharing God's *good news* with people led to the establishment of at least twelve store-front *Missions* in five boroughs in New York City, Long Island, Babylon and Patchogue, L.I.

This may explain why more than 800 people filed by his casket in three days. From the New York Police Department, soldiers, church officials and members, many stood in line, at attention, in loving tribute to this true "Soldier of the Cross."

And that is not the end of his ministry. Besides the hundreds of young men and women responding to his challenge to serve God and people, there is *his family,* all of whom, sooner or later embraced the Christian faith. Whether in business, pastors, teachers, or? They tended to excel in their field, somewhere in the world. It would take a whole book to write a history of them all, but let me share the little I have learned in a short time.

Vincent, the firstborn, followed the printing business, like his father. Son number two, James, became a missionary to China where he and his wife served with great effectiveness for 43 years. Henry, son number three, was a photo engraver in the printing industry. Ninety-year old Tony, (fourth in the line-up) was a powerful "Preacher of the Word" since young manhood, on the streets or in store-front missions. Tony organized and built churches from N.Y. to Indiana. He received Jesus as his "Savior and Lord" at age eight at a children's summer camp in Stormville, N.Y. Some years later, he says he was 'baptized in the Holy Spirit.' It doesn't take long being around him to believe every word of that! Whether on the golf course, shuffleboard court, pool room, or wherever you find him, you'll notice by his conversation that his interest is pretty evenly divided between the joy of his continuing walk with God and his love for family. He has two sons, two daughters, seven grandchildren and nine great-grandchildren! His preparation for the ministry included Beulah Heights Bible School in New Jersey. The last church he served as pastor was in Gary, Indiana.

Tony organized the church there in Gary, and personally oversaw the erection of the large building that would seat 485. He reminded those who worked on it that it was *a holy Temple of the Lord* they were building, and demanded they treat it as such! He served effectively there for 43 years and was known all over the city and state. He was loved and respected by those who knew him. He and his wife lived in Florida some years following retirement. After her death, he moved to Grace Village in Winona Lake, Indiana, near several members of his family.

Joseph, the fifth son, worked for J. J. Little Company in New York City. Sixth in line, Mary, married an Italian preacher. They both excelled as *Preachers of God's Word,* serving their church and God's Kingdom effectively.

Seventh, John, served three years in the mid-East as a reporter of Court Marshals in the Persian Gulf Command. Upon discharge, he became a student at Central Bible College, Springfield, MO, and later at Houghton College, Houghton, N.Y. He majored in Bible and Psychology. He had a minor in French, Social Studies and Language Arts. Upon graduation he taught in public schools, the Elementary Division, for 30 years. He is now retired, and serving as an Elder in his church and sings bass in the choir.

Daniel, number eight, graduated from Central Bible College in Springfield, MO., majored in music and served as Minister of Music at Hollywood Presbyterian Church in California for many years.

Esta, ninth and youngest daughter, was a "career girl" the early part of which she was active in church teaching Sunday School, then met and married a New York City police officer. After several years he came down with congestive heart failure and passed away five years ago. Esta says: "I feel my mother's prayers followed me all my life." Then she said: "Three and one-half years ago I met a wonderful man now retired after serving as pastor of First Presbyterian Church in Allenton, N.J. for 32 years.

He is such a loving man! He tenderly cared for his former wife, who was an Alzheimer's patient, for eight years."

Samuel, number 10, and the youngest, died at age 2 in an epidemic that swept New York City.

Perhaps some day someone can take the time to do further research on the family and labors of Frank Paul Vigna and his wife Rosa Russo. They will probably discover a *large bag full* of real *Diamonds* rather than a couple hands full of "sparklers" that I have found. I love diamonds! They're fascinating. They are among the most valuable and useful jewels in the world. They are created under extreme *heat* and *pressure*. Most of us try hard to avoid those two things in our lives in a effort to live longer on earth.

Thanks to you who have gone back with me to 1885 to pick up and carefully view just a few real *diamonds* in one of the great cities of the world where many valuable jewels get lost and are, unfortunately, never found or widely known. But these are *real people* I have found and come to know and appreciate this past year right here *at home in Indiana!* (A grandson of Tony runs *Digs' Diner* in Warsaw on the Courthouse Square!) His name sounds a bit Italian; Bill DeGaetano! Some—whether it's a claim or a blame, say he makes the world's hottest chili! I have no idea as to its truth. His 'mild' one is plenty hot for me!

What a privilege to know a family through whom the great Creator, Himself, has worked to accomplish His will and purpose! The Vignas believe firmly that *family* was—and is-God's idea. One of the *biggest* and *best* ideas God ever had!

The Vigna family is scattered near and far on God's good earth. Those who know them best will tell you confidently that the world is a much better place to live because of this *one family*—that of Frank Paul and Rosa (Russo) Vigna. They were *mined in Manhattan;* then cut, polished, set and did their sparkling in many parts of the U.S.A. and of the world.

Most Gratefully,

—J. Robert Boggs, Jr. Editor
and
R. Anthony Vigna

The Vigna Family
Back Row: James, Joseph, Daniel, Henry, and Vincent
Middle Row: Frank Paul and Rosa
Front Row: John, Esta, Mary and Anthony "Tony"
Samuel, Dec. 2 yrs. old.

5

A Changed Heart and a Changed Life

—FRANK J. BEARD

I TELL EVERYONE that my mom and dad quit having children when they got the one they wanted. I can say that because I am the baby of the family. Actually, I'm the baby of the two last babies. I have a twin brother who was born minutes before I arrived into the world.

The world was not so kind and open to African Americans in the late fifties. My folks were sharecroppers in rural Arkansas. We were so poor that the roaches had to go next door to eat. We were so poor that I only had one stripe in my pajamas. Truthfully, we were poor but we did not know it because everyone around us shared the same fate.

My folks did the best they could in raising us. Their educational limitations did not stop them from encouraging their children to attend school. They saw education as a way out of poverty and a way "up" in society. Mamma had a sixth grade education but Daddy never learned to read or write, except to print out his name.

As a child growing up it was required that we attend church. Church was never optional. We were not sent to church either. Mom and Dad were at the church with us. My mother taught Sunday School and Daddy was a deacon. The spiritual seeds that were planted at an early age would prove, later on, to be the most significant investment my parents would make in my life. Mom and Dad left rural Arkansas when I was in the fourth grade. We moved to Elkhart, Indiana. My father worked a variety of menial jobs to support the family. My mother worked as a cook at Jack's Café. We were free from "slavery" of share-cropping but we were still poor. There were times Dad would lament the decision to move north because he could not "work the land" or "raise crops."

I found myself a fairly confused kid. I talked with a "down south" country twang. I dressed funny (mostly hand-me-downs or rummage cast-offs). I did not know where to fit in or who to associate with. I was not sure where the lines were any more. In the south it was easy. Black folks stayed with black folks and white folks stayed with white folks. I went to an all-black school, all-black church, lived in an all-black "shanty" neighborhood, and we shopped on the black side of town (even though the stores were owned by whites, it was clearly the "black" side of town). My *new* environment was racially integrated and I was not sure how to handle it.

Imagine my surprise when an older white gentleman invited my brother and me to come inside of their church. It was the promise of cookies and Kool-Aid that lured us out of our "comfort zones." We learned that the church was having a week of something called "Vacation Bible School" and that if we would come, we could get cookies and Kool-Aid every day. We even had a person from the church volunteer to provide transportation. What a deal!

At the end of the week this same gentleman asked us if we would be interested in attending an elementary age summer camp. We told him we were *sure* we could *not* afford to go to camp. He assured us that if our parents gave the "okay" and *if* we wanted to go, the church would pay all of the expenses. That situation quickly turned into a "no-brainer."

I still remember the Wednesday night of that first summer camp. It was called "commitment night." I had no clue what that meant. The camp leader gave a talk about how much Jesus loved us. He told us that God had a special plan for our lives. He told us that we needed to make a "decision" to respond to Jesus' love by opening our hearts and inviting him to live inside. He asked for a show of hands of boys and girls who wanted to have Jesus forgive them of their sins and live inside their hearts. I'm not sure how many other children responded to that invitation, but I did. I prayed a prayer inviting Jesus to live in my life. (I still get goose bumps when I think about that experience.)

I had attended church for years with my folks. I had heard countless sermons. Spiritual "seeds" had been planted in my life at home and in church with my folks, but that night I gave my heart to Jesus and my faith became real. My whole life changed. My attitude, my motivations, my friendships, my self-awareness, and my self-confidence.

I went back to that little church on Division Street a changed kid. The folks there heard that I had given my heart to Jesus at camp. Most of them were excited about that decision. They hugged me and treated me as if I had made the best decision of my life. I had!

Today I am an ordained elder in the United Methodist Church. I have been pastoring for twenty-one years. The greatest day of my life was the day that Jesus took my dirty heart and transformed it into a heart that sparkles with His redeeming love. I praise the Lord for taking a rural country boy and changing his life with the good news of Jesus Christ. God does take **coal** and "turn it into diamonds!" *Editor's Note:* When Dr. Frank J. Beard was still in college and theological seminary, I was pastor of his home church in Elkhart, Indiana, and had the joy of assisting in his marriage to Melissa! Now, in barely two decades, I have eagerly watched him develop into a tremendous speaker and shepherd of souls. With befitting humility he does not flout the title "Dr." with his name. More than one member of his church said to me, "Frank Beard is the best preacher I've ever heard speak in my life." It was the day several years ago when I was speaking at the two morning services at his big church when he was away getting the earned "Dr." degree conferred on him. When you remember who and where Frank was in the late 1950's and look at him now, you tend to say "Miracle!" Yes. And God did it! How? Through his parents and many dedicated church people in Arkansas and Indiana and many unknown, unheralded people all over America in one of the "big" denominational churches—**plus** Frank's own hard work and initiative.

Dr. Frank J. Beard

6

Two 1,200-Mile Prayers

From
I Met Them on the Trail

—J. ROBERT BOGGS

IN MAY OF 1952 we moved from the austere climate of western North Dakota to the relatively moderate one of Ft Wayne, Indiana. By late summer my wife Maxine and I had found a good pediatrician for our four small children, the able and friendly Dr. Scott. He was checking the immunization status of our Bobby, 7; Betty, 6; Carol, 5; and our cat-loving toddler, Barbara, 2.

"So you moved to Ft. Wayne to be closer to family in nearby Ohio and have fewer blizzards to fight in winter. Tell me," said Dr. Scott, " what did you like most about the west?"

"The people were the big plus. I found the spirit of adventure that lured early settlers west still alive. When they encountered the rigors of life on the frontier they had to stick together to survive. The 40-below temps chilled my Georgia blood, but each blizzard I took as a new challenge. Everywhere was miles away—wide open spaces."

"Interesting," said Dr. Scott. "We hoosiers could use more strength-building helps here where we live closer together but are often short on the spirit of caring.

"I've heard there's good hunting out on those prairies.Did you go hunting?"

"Oh, yes! I got my first deer on the 13,000 acre ranch of one of my church members. Ranches teem with pheasants and grouse. Antelope, too. Whatever you want is not too far away. It's almost a hunter's paradise."

Dr. Scott's face began to light up. "Could you take me hunting out on that ranch?"

"Why not?" I said. "How soon do you want to go? This fall?"

"Wow! Are you serious? I'm ready right now! Do you think we could do it?"

"You bet! I'll get in touch with my friends at the Hall ranch, at Trotters, North Dakota, and let you know as soon as I find out."

Thus the fall adventure began. Soon I had the needed information and our plans began to take shape. We've heard it said: "Half the fun of a journey is planning it." Anticipation had no lack in this trip. One day I got a call from Dr. Scott. "Bob, I have a good doctor friend who needs to get away. As a doctor of internal medicine, he's one of the best. But his success seems to push him toward being a workaholic. My question: Could we, by any chance, take him along with us? He has a big station wagon we could use. It would hold a lot of game."

"Why not?" I replied without hesitation, and Dr. "Aubrey" was included. The game plan was to hunt antelope at a ranch along the Tongue River in eastern Montana; thence to the Hall ranch near Trotters, North Dakota, for grouse and pheasants. A couple weeks before we were to head west, Dr. Scott called with an unusual request.

"Bob, since Montana is about 1,200 miles, would you join me in a 1,200 mile prayer? I'm suggesting that we pray all that way for my dear friend, Aubrey. He has no personal religious faith. He's a great guy. I think all he needs is to come to know our Savior, the Lord Jesus. He is not an atheist, but an agnostic. He says he just does not know if there's a God. It's a bit hard to talk to him about it, but let's ask God to open his heart to real "life". Perhaps one of us will have the chance to talk to him about it."

"Yes, my brother, I will be glad to join you in such a prayer. What a great idea! Along with you, I find that being a Christian is a real adventure all the way." Thus the stage was set.

The trip to Montana was beautiful, and we even got our antelope! Then back to Trotters, North Dakota, where we found pheasants and grouse plentiful. Grouse is a hard bird to hit! Their noisy, surprise "B-29 bomber takeoff" tends to shake the nerves of the steadiest hunter. But we got our limit of everything. Reluctantly, we came to our last night around the friendly fireside of the old log ranch house with the big Hall family.

The women prepared a memorable farewell feast that night, after which we gathered in the big living room in the sprawling old house. Grandpa Hall, the patriarch of the whole family, asked me, their former pastor, to baptize one of his grand-children and read some scriptures for a devotional and prayer before we retire. The impromptu sermon was not real long, but the length of the singing (to the accompaniment of the old pump organ) was long enough to make up for my brevity. What a wonderful, sweet spirit in this unre-hearsed "extended family worship!" Made it hard to close it and go to bed. Just an old-fashioned family, with invited guests, enjoying their Christian faith together!

Next morning "Mother Hall" was up long before daylight, seeing to it that we had a hardy ranch-hand breakfast before we forded Wildcat Creek in our big station wagon stuffed with our gear and game to begin our long trip home to Indiana.

For the first leg of the homeward journey, Dr. Scott napped atop the "stuff" in the back while Dr. Aubrey drove. I was to see that he stayed awake. We negotiated the 40 miles of ranch roads and gravel highway down to cross-country highway US 10 before dawn. I took the opportunity to quietly talk to Dr. Aubrey. I hoped to share with him something of my religious experience and give him a chance to share his thoughts.

"Aubrey," I said, "do you ever remember any time in you life when God spoke to you and you recognized it as such?"

"Nope," he replied with no hesitation. "Never remember any experience like that."

"That's unusual," I replied. "I've talked with hundreds of people in my first ten years as a pastor, and I've never had anyone tell me that. I've always believed that God loves everybody, and makes an effort to communicate personally with them."

I let the subject rest, but not for long. "Do you mean to say that in nearly fifty years of life you don't remember a moment of *awe* or *wonder* when your heart suddenly beat faster and you sensed the presence of "someone" reasoning with you, or drawing you?"

Everything got quiet for a while. Eventually, Dr. Aubrey spoke up and said, "Well, I just remembered something. Last night—while you guys were reading, talking and singing along with that old pump organ out at the ranch—my heart began to beat faster, and I got a lump in my throat that I couldn't get up or down for a long time. I never, in my whole life, remember any experience quite like it."

"Aubrey!" I said, "*that* is what I was talking about! I call that 'the call of The Parent to a child!' I believe God, at least once, gives every human a 'come home' call like that. I heard and felt that call when I was twelve. I heard it clear as a bell at age 17, but this time I courageously said 'yes' rather than my usual 'no' or 'later'. And, I will forever be glad I did. I can't tell you the joy, peace, and true happiness that *one* decision started!"

Sensing that Dr. Aubrey had shared all he wished to for the present, I let the subject drop at that point and pretty soon we were coming into the Teddy Roosevelt National Park, about 30 miles east of Beach, North Dakota, as the eastern sky slowly began to get lighter, then turn various shades of red as the gigantic ball of fire slipped from behind a thin row of dark clouds, then upwards into a pale-blue sky.

Though a little tired from the long ride home, renewed and refreshed would certainly be accurate words to describe the feeling of the three of us men when we arrived home in Ft. Wayne to resume our occupations.

*   *   *

About five years later I was at a banquet where a panel of doctors made a presentation to the group. I was happy to see my friend, Dr. Scott, was one of the group on the stage. When the program ended, I made my way to him. Soon I asked this question: "And how is Dr. Aubrey?"

"Yes, Bob, that is what I wanted to share with you. Not long ago he came down with cancer of the throat and after a not too long siege, he died. But the *good news* is that before he died, he turned his life over to our Lord Jesus, and became a real testimony for our God. He still loved his work, and continued to see patients up until a few days before his home-going. I've been eager to see you and report that wonderful answer to our 1,200 mile prayers to North Dakota and eastern Montana. Yes! God is good—all the time!"

7

Along the Trail III

From
The Canadian Great North Woods

RUSSELL W. SMITH

ERVIN SMITH and his wife, Lucinda Leemon Smith, were married and set up housekeeping 80 miles north of Kingston, Ontario, Canada. There I, Russell W., oldest of four children, was born. When I was seven years old I started to a one-room school at Fernleigh. Imagine a seven year old boy walking six miles round trip five days a week through deep woods that served as home for lynx, bears, and wolves!

One very cold morning I stopped a half-mile down the trail at my aunt's house to thaw my frozen fingers before walking the other 2-1/2 miles. The heavy mitts my mother made didn't keep out the biting Canadian chill that morning! I soon learned to keep my hands deep inside my pockets.

The next year Dad heard of a job cutting wood to fire the boilers at a graphite mine 40 miles north at a place called Black Donald Mine. We lived only two miles from the village and school, but when I reported seeing a wolf track in the snow, my mother decided my safety was more important that schooling for the present.

My mother and dad decided to room and board two men who worked at the mine, so mother cooked for an enlarged family while doing all the knitting of socks and mittens for her family. She must have fit the description of the "virtuous woman" spoken of in Proverbs 31. She needed a sewing machine to speed up the making of clothes for her family, so she cut many cords of wood to earn the $25.00 cash needed.

When I was ten, the family moved again. This time for Dad to work as a maintenance man in the Golden Fleece gold mine at Flinton, Ontario. The next summer the Smiths moved back "down home" 40 miles, and were busy picking wild berries to sell. People would drive as far as 25 miles to buy them. I was 11 then, and picked $60.00 worth of blueberries, which sold for 75 cents per 8-quart pail. That's a lot of berries! It was two miles up to the mountain where the berries grew, and Dad made a yoke to carry two 8-quart pails, plus a pail in each hand—32 quarts of berries per trip down from the mountain berry patch where we picked them!

When I was fourteen I did the work of a man at one end of a crosscut saw I had a cousin who was a guard at the Kingston Prison, and at fifteen I was plowing like a man—and so proud of myself that I could do it! Mother taught me to worship and Dad taught me to work, and everything seemed to be moving smoothly for the Smiths. That is, until that December 21 morning when I was returning from my trap line. I looked up to see the peak of the roof of our house erupting bright red flames. Our house was burning! And burn it did, leaving nothing but ashes. We lost nearly everything we had. We almost lost my baby brother! Mother carried him out of the bedroom just as the ceiling fell in! I was 15 years old when my brother was born, thus we never had the privilege of playing together like other brothers. When I was only four, I worked hard helping Mother pull weeds in the garden. Maybe I pulled more than weeds!

I recall my sister and I walking a mile to school near Flinton, Ontario. There was a boy in that school who was mean! He was always picking on me—until my sister hit him with the dinner pail! After that he left me alone and walked by himself.

We lived in my uncle's house for the winter and started building in the spring—on the old foundation. We moved in that fall, and were glad to be back in our own home.

About that time in my life I started to prayerfully think about what I should be doing for a life occupation. I read in a magazine about a company in Toronto that offered a course in sign painting and show card writing. At the completion of the course they would send me work by mail. I enrolled, completed the course and got my diploma. They sent me work for about two years and the company went bankrupt.

I had a cousin who was a guard at the Kingston Penitentiary. He said the government was building another prison only three miles from Kingston. I sent my application in, and waited three years. Finally, I got a letter from the warden asking me to report for duty! I did, in 1933—right in the "great depression." When I boarded the train I little realized the different kind of life I was headed for. I went on night duty for a 13-hour shift. Two of us guards were in a dormitory with 50 convicts. After five years, I joined the engineering department.

To advance I would have to study very hard, but with my wife's help in math, I got the degree I needed for a better job.

Billy, A Sad-Happy Story

Let me share with you a sad-happy story from my work with prisoners. Truth, at times, is stranger than fiction. "Billy" lived with his widowed mother. They were having a hard time making it. To protect the innocent, let's call him "Billy." Sadly, the mother sent seven-year old Billy out to steal. With her instruction, he came home with his pockets full of little things like tooth paste, apples, oranges, etc. Finally, Billy graduated to the "big stuff." He and his pals decided to rob a bank. Billy was undecided at first, but for a boy in his late teens he thought it was time to begin to "get ahead" and maybe become a "big shot." So they planned it carefully. Billy would drive the getaway car, and one of the other guys would go into the bank, point a gun at the teller, and demand money. The poor girl who was the teller was scared stiff. She gave him a big roll of bills, and out he walked to the getaway car. No problem!

Most anyone could guess how the next move went. Someone was shot, and died. One young man got the death penalty, and Billy got life imprisonment. To help fill up his time, Billy got interested in making fishing lures. A Christian business man heard about Billy and visited him. He knew a Christian man who operated a bait and tackle store in northern Canada. He had him contact Billy, who was finally paroled into his care. He gave his life to Christ and continued to work in the store up north. One day Billy met a lady at the store—a widow with three children. They fell in love and got married. I heard Billy say in a speech he was giving at a church: "God gave me a ready-made family."

The last I heard, Billly and his wife had established a half-way house for ex-cons with a high success rate in leading them to Christ and a useful life. He was grateful for the chance God and His children gave him to a *new life* so he wants to help give that same "new start" in life to others that was given to him. That's the story of Billy. Every story could end "and they all lived happy lives thereafter" if only we humans had wisdom enough to consistently make right choices.

Personally, "going on 93," I want to thank God for my Christian mother. She would read the Bible every day and, out of respect for her, we would all get on our knees while she prayed. Dad was finally "saved" before he died. But look at all the good, happy and delightful things he missed by waiting so long!

After turning my life over to Christ Jesus at age 13, I'm sorry to confess that I did not stay as close to Him, nor walk with Him like I should. But God's marvelous grace protected me from deep sin. For this, I am deeply grateful!

But after my first wife and I were happily married, we both surrendered our lives to Jesus Christ at the church we had chosen, and were filled with the Holy Spirit. Furthermore, my wife was healed of cancer. I have been elected to serve on the boards and councils of our local church numerous times throughout the years, always counting it a privilege.

After a long and beautiful marriage to my first wife that was terminated by a relentless onslaught of cancer, I was devastated and felt I could die from grief. God surprised me again when one February, I flew to a place called "**Christian Retreat**" near Bradenton, Florida, where I met a dedicated Christian lady who has beautifully filled the empty *void* in my life with sweet fellowship and joyous companionship!

Surely, my "mother's prayers have followed me" just as the song says. I feel so sorry for all the boys and girls who do not have a praying mother! (See pictures in Appendix.)

8

Epitaph for a Daughter with Acknowledgment to a Loving God Who Took Her Back

—Stephen and Ginny Saint

Dear extended family,

Ginny and I want to thank you for caring for us during a very intense time in our lives. I would have said "a difficult time" but that is not really descriptive of what we are experiencing after the sudden death of our dear daughter Stephenie Raquel "Nemo" Saint. Instead, this is what we would call a "happy-sad time."

The Bible which we have chosen as our "rule of faith and conduct" says that we should give thanks in all things (1Th.5:18a.) It also says, in one of my favorite passages, "Trust in the Lord with all your heart; in all your ways acknowledge Him and He will direct your ways." (Prov. 3:5–6.) I have always wondered how you can give thanks when things happen that are so painful that they tear your heart apart. Now we know something about that. Ginny and I want to "acknowledge God" by giving you just a thumb-nail sketch of what we have been facing.

We have four children, the last of which is our only girl. She was tall with long blond hair; just turned 20 this month. She was an excellent student, never brought home anything but "A's." She was enrolled as a piano performance major at the Univ. of Florida so we got to see her every week-end until this last year which she spent traveling with a Christian music group called "Carpenter's Tools."

Steph's year of traveling ended a week ago, Sat., July 22, 2000. We got the gang together—including one of our two brand-new granddaughters—and went to the airport to meet her. We all made "welcome home" signs with her name so we could properly embarrass her as she came off the plane in Orlando. She played along, pretending she didn't know us but it was abundantly obvious that our little girl was glad to be home. We piled the family, including Tementa and Mincaye (they are both elders from the Huaorani tribe that killed dad (Nate Saint) and his four buddies in January 1956 and with whom aunt Rachel—for whom Stephenie Raquel is partly named—spent so much of her life.) They are here with us in Florida because I was invited to participate with them in "Amsterdam 2000," the world-wide conference for itinerant evangelists, the beginning of August.

We got home and started our "welcome home" party. All was well with the world. Our little girl was back in our care! She was well and happy and terribly excited about her two nieces. Steph loved anything that was helpless or "down and out." Babies were #1 on her short list of favorite things and God had just given us two with one on the way; just so this would be the happiest place in the world for her, I was sure. We were looking forward to having our, "intense, stimulating, up or down but never dull" little girl in the middle of our lives after the only protracted absence ever.

What can I say? "Life was good, cup running over full, if it gets any better I'll explode, wonderful." Then, Steph got a headache. She started to cry, saying "It feels like I'm being hit in the head with a hammer." Ginny called me in to pray for her. I did, and she had a mild seizure and lost consciousness— all in about five minutes. I called 911 and rode in the ambulance with her. They "intubated" her. We were in a modern hospital within minutes and surely this couldn't be anything more than a letdown after an intense trip where she had lots of responsibilities and little sleep. The doctor wanted a CAT scan and then said: "She is young and healthy but with injuries such as this, she is a very sick young lady."

Surely there was a major misunderstanding; she had suffered no injury; she just had a little Ibuprofen, "take two pills and it's gone" headache.

That is when we started to learn about some of the promises that our "Rule Book" makes for those who submit to its author. I felt a sense of *peace* come over me that is neither natural nor normal. The medical staff did the evaluations; hooked our little girl's beautiful, pure body up to the monitors and pumps. But it was clear that God was in charge and we quickly relaxed. He took Steph—we liked to call her *Dolly*—some time during the night. The medical staff very efficiently kept her pretty shell alive until Sunday afternoon. I dreaded every step of the long ordeal we had to go through:

1. We had to come to grips with the fact that she was dying while she showed no evidence of any injury; she just had a headache. I knew God could raise her up. I could picture her sitting up in the hospital bed and *screaming* because some stranger had cut off her clothes and underwear, leaving her covered only with a flimsy hospital gown. (It is amazing

that hospitals have the best of everything but can't ever seem to get patient gowns that even pretend to be modest of fit, and always old and threadbare!)

I could just see us all crying with joy. We'd have bought three gallons of Prestige's best burgundy cherry ice cream and would have finished the happiest and most grateful "welcome home party" ever.

I not only believed God could do it, but I even believed He would, if we asked Him to; but we couldn't. We knew He had a purpose and we have seen Him work through enough hurts and difficulties that we were confident that this was *His doing*. We knew we were seeing "Plan A" being acted out. If we asked God to give Steph back we would have moved to "Plan B." Our hearts were being torn out by the roots; we were in the agony of *surprise* and *helplessness,* but we felt a sense of peace and wellbeing that can only be understood by those who have experienced it.

It has always been my privilege to be Dolly's protector. Suddenly I was helpless. Ginny has always been Stephenie's best friend and confidant, but Steph couldn't talk to her. And yet we both knew that God was not only taking her from us; He was taking her from a world full of "people-hurting-people-and ignoring-God." Both of these hurt Steph, at least when it was professing Christians who were living "outside the bounds." I had to protect my little girl from this terrible thing that was taking her from us; I was *desperate* to do something. And then I saw that it was her *perfect* heavenly Father—the one who had given her to us for 20 years and 20 days who was taking her. I knew that she no longer had to feel responsible for the world's shortcomings. She would no longer feel *isolated* in her desire to live a morally pure and spiritually responsible life in a world pressing in other directions.

In May, Steph wrote in her journal in response to a disappointment with a close friend: "I got angry and sad and hurt all over again. Sometimes the longing for complete security is so great that I can't hold back the tears. I know that complete fulfillment can only be found in God, but it's hard to just give myself up to that. Maybe I am wrong and everyone else is right when they say it's ridiculous to feel the way I do (about the importance of moral purity.) I can only pray that this is part of God's plan to strengthen me for something down the line. I want a life that's more than just being an ordinary woman going from day to day with no larger goal. I need something that will stimulate my mind and make me feel productive for God."

We believe Steph now has the answers to "why bad things happen to good people," why evil so often seems to triumph over good; why people choose their own way when it is so evident that the end of that road is emptiness. We are confident that she is completely secure in the presence of God's perfect and unconditional love. We are not disappointed that God has taken her. This is the end of that toward which we have been **coaxing** her for 20 precious years. We are just surprised by the timing and grieving for *our* loss. We would like to negotiate weekend visits, but we wouldn't have her back. We love her and our heavenly Father too much for that.

We dreaded the reality that God could—and probably was—taking her; that He didn't need our approval or cooperation to do so. When He finally did, I felt an almost *euphoric* sense of *well-being*. I sensed that our children are like our players on a board game. The objective is to get them all "home." On the board there are numerous spaces that are dangerous; go to jail, go back some spaces, lose a turn, and the like. My strategy in such a game is to pick one of my players at a time and get them safely home. As soon as we knew *God* was *taking* our dear sweet girl, he let me see that she was *home safe*.

2. Ginny and I have regularly taken a direction in raising our children that has put us out of sync with most of the world around us. We have grown quite independent of the standards and fads that have come and gone in our North American culture. In the process, I have grown protective of my position as head of this precious family of ours. I dreaded having to trust strangers to make life-and-death decisions for our little girl. On the other hand, I also dreaded the possibly negative reaction I would risk if I *challenged* the professional medical staff who were being required to make critical decisions on a fire drill schedule in the middle of the night. But God met our need before we knew it existed. The neurologist who attended us was of Latin origin and won our confidence immediately. One of our family members noticed the neurosurgeon, who was on call and came to evaluate the possibility of emergency surgery, on his knees in the chapel as we (not Steph) were hanging between emotional life and death.

The surgical Intensive Care nurses allowed us to shuttle family members between the family waiting room and Steph's critical care bedside with almost no limitations. As our family grew to fill the entire waiting room, it was impossible for us to differentiate between those who were family by the hospital standards and those who have become family through their incredible and selfless love for us. As each decision had to be made, I, who would normally and instinctively have felt a need to control the fate of my little girl and to protect her, felt perfectly at ease to entrust all the medical decisions to the medical staff.

At Steph's bedside we felt a peace that passes understanding. In the SICU waiting room we sang "Holy Spirit, You are welcome in this place" and we felt His presence in our hearts. The dread that we anticipated did not materialize. Instead, we achieved hugging status with a number of the SICU staff and Steph's first shift attending nurse came to her funeral, along with his fiancee.

3. As news of Steph's condition began to come to us and we agonized over hope, not knowing whether to hold on or let go, I began to feel that her Heavenly Father was ready to take my sweet girl back for Himself. I couldn't bear to let go but I didn't dare to hold on. Then I agonized over what to tell Ginny. I realized that even one wrong word at a time like this can drive a wedge between loved ones. My greatest agony then and now was to realize that my opportunity to transition from my primary role as "policeman" to that of "friend" was never going to come. I was convinced that I would never get to show her my "soft side." And then, just as clearly as you are reading this father's account of my heart-wrenching grief, I felt God assuring me that *all would be well.*

I remembered Steph's last Father's Day card, sent to me just before she left Minnesota for Trinidad. She wrote, "I often tend to see the tough side of you, Pop, and forget that you sometimes feel weak and vulnerable too. It was so good for me to see the tender side of you; to see that your heart gets wounded and your eyes cry just like mine. Thank you so much for the example of Godliness that your life has been for me, no matter if my friends turned away or everyone else rejected me, I would still have love and acceptance at home. I need more than a father/daughter relationship with you. I want us to be friends. Not many others understand us and how we think, so we'd better stick together, huh?"

4. Can you imagine how I dreaded having the topic of organ donation brought up? I had only considered it in relation to my own body, and had a difficult time imagining signing my organs away to be used in strangers. But suddenly it was a hundred times worse to think of a total stranger asking me to allow him to take parts of our lovely daughter while her heart was still beating and her beautiful body was still warm!

A stranger approached me in the SICU hallway and I knew who he was. But in the instant where I thought my heart would fail for sure, God suddenly opened my mind to a new thought. Steph, who had taken such good care of her body, would now be able to give a chance for life to several other people. My dread was replaced with an actual *yearning* to see her healthy organ go, possibly to someone else's daughter who was dying; possibly to someone who did not have the hope we have for true life after death. I just kept remembering Steph's comment when we were evaluating the cost and return of her spending a year traveling with her singing group. She kept saying, "If just one person's life is changed, won't that be enough?"

The forms were endless; medications used? "None." Not even birth control? Ginny heard this one, and left Steph's bed long enough to tell him, "the only man Steph ever kissed was her Daddy."

"How about recreational drugs?"

"No chance" came our answer.

I could tell that this man was not relishing the responsibility of asking us these questions with our daughter just a few feet away. I thought I could help him out. I realized that all parents must think their children are quite innocent and this man knew that few really were. So I assured him: "I know many parents don't know the personal and intimate activities their children are involved in. We have worked with young people for years, and we *are* realists. But with *this* young lady, and on the truth of her having lived a pure life, I would stake my own life on it."

The kind man looked at me differently after that. Either we were deluded and extremely naïve or we had a very *different* kind of relationship with a *very special* daughter! When his report came back he had added a very nice note: "Your daughter's body was a beautiful example of clean living." We were thankful for even this small opportunity to give a testimony, and I remembered again:

"If just one person's life is changed, won't that be enough?"

5. I have often rebelled at the complexity of our society. In most parts of the world, when you die you just have to die. In Ecuador you have only 24 hours to bury your dead. Here, there are interminable decisions to make and I dreaded having to go through that. What funeral home to use? What cemetery? Metal or wood coffin? Prices range from $20,000 (from what I considered the stratosphere) down to $3,000. Do you want a vault with a single liner or a double liner, sealing or non-sealing? Even the outsides of the vaults are decorated—decorations you will never ever see. At I-TEC we could produce *five complete dental operatories* for the cost of one of the *least expensive* coffins! I could hardly stand it.

I had told Steph, when we were in the jungles together, how much I liked aunt Rachel's plain plywood coffin made by one of the Mission Aviation Fellowship pilots—cost about $12.00 told her *that* was what I wanted to be buried in and she told me she wanted the same. But here—and now—the only pine box available at the funeral home was a cremation box that cost several thousand dollars. Ginny took the matter out of my hands by telling me she wanted the oak one. (At the funeral I was reminded that we aren't the only ones who are grieving over Stephenie.) I would have preferred a plywood box of my own making, but it would not have satisfied the expectations of our enormous "extended family." Once again *my heart was comforted.*

As Stephenie slipped deeper and deeper into a coma, I mentioned that I kept imagining her sitting up and asking to go home. I knew that we would have been the most grateful people in the world and we would have had the rip-roaringest party ever. But that wasn't God's plan. He took our Dolly from us, *but He gave us such a sense of well being* and reminded us so much of His deep love—not only for Stephenie but also for us—that after we walked her body down to have her final surgery, we came home and had a party anyway! To some that might seem almost morbid; and I would hesitate to mention it IF I didn't know that many of you who will read this have felt that there are *different remedies* our loving Heavenly Father metes out to His children when they go through troubles and trials.

Ginny and I like to sing a song that has been coming to mind very frequently these last few days. It goes like this: "We are so blessed by the gifts from Your hand, we just can't understand why You loved us so much. We are so blessed—take what we have to bring; take it all, everything; Lord we give it to you."

6. It wasn't what happened to our sweet daughter that caught us by surprise and caused us to grieve. It was the timing of it all. One minute she was walking around the house carrying her beautiful two-month-old niece, and inserting herself into every activity and every conversation—she was inserting

herself back into our lives in typical Stephenie, *full speed ahead* fashion. Five minutes later she was crying out in pain and then lost consciousness in Ginny's arms while the family accompanied me in praying for God to relieve her headache so she could enjoy the excitement of our *welcome home* celebration.

There was nothing to remind us that she wasn't really "home." We sing "This world is not my home; I'm just a-passing through . . . " We believe it, but our sense of reality is warped. We believe we are just passing through but we count on a *slow passage.*

Actually, life isn't a gift; it's a *loan.* God called this, *His loan,* in and we were temporarily caught off guard.

God's Timing

Consider His timing with me for a minute. If this was an arterial venal malformation as the doctors suspect, she might have died at any time since she was born. So we started to be more thankful for the 20 years and 20 days! On the way home from the airport we stopped to pick up Ginny' s car and Steph wanted to drive. She had Ginny and our dear daughter-in-law, along with our brand new granddaughter, with her. *What if* she had passed out *then* and they had all been killed? *What if* it had happened a day earlier and she had been in Minnesota? We could have spent hours on the plane wondering who was taking charge, wondering if everything possible was being done for her. *If* it had been *two days* before, and she had died in Trinidad, and would likely have had to be buried before we could even have gotten to her! You can *imagine* our relief and *thanksgiving* to a loving and gracious heavenly Father who brought her back to her temporal home and to her earthly mother and father, brothers and sisters-in-law and friends, before taking her to her *"real"* home! "God is good all the time; All the time God is good!"

7. I wanted to take Steph home from the hospital so we could celebrate. God took her, but He made it possible for us to go celebrate anyway. God took our Dolly home sometime early Sunday morning. On Tuesday evening we invited family and friends to the funeral home to see her body. In our "death denying age" we call it a "viewing" I guess.

Well, this was more of a *singing* than a viewing; or maybe I should call it a, *"singing and praying and hugging."* They gave us the chapel at the funeral home because I had asked if we could have a piano. We must have had over 300 people come by to spend time with us.

We did a fair bit of crying, but we did a lot more singing and praying and hugging. I had an opportunity to apologize to an old friend for a grievance I had held against him for years. That was the first memorial I wanted to offer to Steph's memory. God opened up the door.

Dear old grandfather Mincaye, one of the men who killed Steph's grandfather, looked at Stephenie's body lying in the casket and asked: "Did the doctor do something to hurt her?" I realized that in this plastic, fantastic world that is so radically different from his jungle home he must have thought we had taken Steph to the hospital in the truck with all the lights as part of some ceremony or pageant. The next thing he knew, his "granddaughter" was lying in a casket, dead.

I felt terrible that I hadn't explained more completely and tried to tell him all that was happening was new to us, too. "Nemo (the Huarorani gave Stephenie Raquel aunt Rachel's tribal name, which means, "Star") has gone to heaven. All we know is that Wan-gongui, the Creator, wanted her to come." Mincaye understood. He said "let's talk to God." First he began to speak to all the foreigners gathered with us in the chapel. "We are all going to God's place when we die. I am an old man now, and I will be going soon. We must all walk God's trail *very carefully* so we don't get lost, then, following very carefully we will see Nemo and Nemo-woodi (Aunt Rachel, woodi, who has already died) and we will see Babae's father (Bagae is what the tribe calls me) and Guikita-woodi . . ." and he went on to name the growing list of people he knew to be in heaven.

Twenty-eight precious young people who have been part of the youth group that met in our home while our four children were growing up came to the viewing and memorial services. What a wonderful opportunity to tell them that the theory about God with us where we are and healing all our hurts if we will trust Him, *wasn't just theory.*

At the memorial service we wanted to have a *celebration*. The funeral director said it would tend to be solemn no matter what we planned. We didn't want to do solemn, however. We wanted to acknowledge God's goodness and love for us. We would have been happy to just have had a few family and friends. Instead, Highlands Baptist Church was packed with family from Minnesota, Michigan, and North Carolina. Friends flew in from all over the country. One of Steph's special friends from her singing group came all the way from Hungary.

Words cannot express the humbling gratitude we feel for the incredible outpouring of love and sympathy we have been immersed in. We didn't get to take Steph home to have the party of gratitude that I could almost feel, I wanted it so badly. Instead, God took His little Dolly "***home.***" We went back to where she has spent so many years of her life and had two wonderful celebrations, remembering the little girl that has—and still holds—such a huge place in our hearts and the loving heavenly Father whose timing was perfect.

At the very end of our celebration ceremony dear friends of *ours* from West Virginia sang an old family favorite of ours: "See the bright lites shine; it's just about home time; I can see my Father standing at the do-oo-or. This world's been a wilderness; I'm ready for deliverance; Lord, I've never been this homesick befo-oo-or." Amen!

Everyone was singing; we were clapping, and there was a little foot stomping going on. I was waiting for someone, overcome with joy, to start dancing in the aisles. I would have joined them! My heart was breaking in grief and bursting with joy at the same time. Go figure!

8. Stephenie's career choice was to be the best wife and mother, ever. She promised us nine grandchildren. She was studying piano so she could help support her anticipated large family if the need arose. It's OK that she won't get a chance to be a wife and mother. The goal of "best" was virtually unattainable because God gave Steph (and Shaun and Jaime and Jesse) a mother—and me a wife that—well, it's hard to imagine she could beat!

But He did give babies to two of the sisters-in-law that she loved. And her other sister-in-law has one on the way. Steph was so excited one would think all this was happening to her! But God gave her the *hope* of romance. She would not date; told all the boys who expressed an interest that they would have to come and talk to me first. I have a feeling she told a few of them that Ginny and I would have to come along.

One young man actually came up and asked me if that was true! I couldn't remember putting quite that stringent a requirement on Steph, but I assured him it was! He told me to expect a visit. At the graveside, Stephenie's special friend from Hungary sang "How Great Thou Art" in Hungarian. He was in love with our Dolly. Another young man said after they lowered her casket into the grave, "Everything I ever dreamed of in a girl was just buried in that hole." Our hearts go out to the many others who will have to re-group their hopes and dreams to conform to what we *now* know is God's plan for Stephenie.

"Heaven is a wonderful pla-ace; Filled with glory and gra-ace; I want to see my Savior's face—And Steph's, and Dad Nate's, and Grandpa Jim's and old Gluikitas and Aunt Rachel's, and. . . . Heaven is a wonderful. Heaven is glorious. Heaven is a wonderful place!!"

9. As we made funeral arrangements I found myself wishing that we could offer our local community in Ocala a glimpse of how God can make devastating sorrow sweet by telling them about Steph's life and commitments. I knew there was no real news in the "passing of one young lady" no matter how lovely and loved she was. I yearned for the opportunity of her death to "make a difference in just one life" here where she has spent most of her life (when we weren't living in Africa or the Amazon jungles.)

At the fellowship dinner after Steph's burial, the pastor handed me his cell 'phone and said it was someone from our local newspaper. "Do you want to talk to her?" he asked. My mind raced to try to figure out if this could possibly be leading up to the fulfillment of that small wish.

The reporter came over to our house with two photographers that evening. We had a house full of family and friends. It wasn't very convenient, but it held promise for an answer to my wish. Before interviewing us, the reporter told us that she knew Stephenie. In 1992 she had been a substitute teacher for Steph's class. The class gave her a very difficult time, but she wanted us to know that Stephenie and one other girl had gone out of their way to obey her. Steph, she said, had been very upset with her classmates and let it be known. Her attitude didn't permeate the class or result in any such happy ending but it was a comforting reminder that our little girl had a tender heart for people who were hurting. Even at that tender age, about 11 or 12, she was willing to stand against the popular flow to do what she thought was right. What a sweet coincidence for God to arrange that the very teacher that Ginny had talked about at the memorial service turned out to be the reporter that came to write about Stephenie's life and death.

I believe that Stephenie's willingness to stand alone for what was right but unpopular would have caused her to suffer a great deal of rejection in life. I am willing to face it myself, but it was hard to think of my little girl suffering through it. She wanted so much to be liked, but compromise was not only *not tempting*—it was virtually impossible.

As the reporter interviewed us, along with Tementa and Mincaye, we were interrupted over and over by telephone calls and people stopping by to console us. I saw the dis-combobulated notes and thought it would be impossible for anyone to write an accurate article from them, much less one with heart.

Friday morning—not in the religion section on Saturday—but right on the front page of the Star Banner which is owned by the New York Times-was the article. Surrounded by two other articles talking about death, one showing a woman nearly collapsing from grief over a loved one killed in the Concord, was a picture of our Stephenie being hugged by two beautiful young girls in Trinidad. Even the fact that they happened to be from a different race comforted my heart. I have yearned for the Black community here in Ocala to know that we are a color-blind family. Here was evidence on the very front page of our paper. Just one more blessing for our happy-sad hearts.

Summary

We grieve because we loved Stephenie with all our hearts, but "we grieve not as those who are without hope." (1 Th. 4:13b) We seem strong but it is God holding us steady that people see. At first we were afraid to move about, worried that we might fall out of His arms. Then we realized that we were not just cradled in His arms, but that He had a hold on us that, "neither tribulation, or distress, or any other thing" can overcome.

"He giveth more strength when the burdens grow greater." Most of the parents we have seen these last days wondered how we could face what God has dealt us. They do not understand—because they haven't yet felt—His loving arms holding them in this position. We hadn't either. But He came to us and lifted us up—just in time!

"God works in mysterious ways His wonders to perform. He plants His feet upon the seas and rides upon the storm. His purposes will ripen fast, unfolding every hour, the bud may have a bitter taste but sweet will be the flower. Blind unbelief is sure to err and search His ways in vain; God is His own interpreter and He will make it plain."—William Cowper. Many Christians are taught to believe that the difference between us and those who don't "believe" is that we have only joy and they have only pain. We know that isn't true. But is there a real difference? Of course there is. The difference is that their joy is superficial because it cannot last beyond death, but their pain is fundamental. It will never end. For us who know Christ as Savior and Lord, our *joy* is fundamental and our pain is temporary. We're feeling it right now! It washes over us in waves and we feel we won't make it back to the surface to see that the sun is shining and the sea is calm even while the storm is raging around us.

We say with the Psalmist in 116:7–15, "Return to your rest, O my soul; For the Lord has dealt bountifully with you. For Thou hast rescued my soul from death, my eyes from tears, my feet from stumbling. I shall walk before the Lord in the land of the living. I believed when I said "I am greatly afflicted." I said in my alarm, "All men are liars." "What shall I render to the Lord for all His benefits toward me? I shall lift up the cup of salvation, and call upon the name of the Lord. I shall pay my vows to the Lord; Oh may it be in the presence of all His people (and it has been.) "Precious in the sight of the Lord is the death of His godly ones!"

We willingly give back to God the wonderful daughter He so generously loaned to us for a season. We thank Him for the three sons, plus three daughters-in-law and two sweet babies, and for the other one who is on the way! When I had candy, it was just like Steph to take it and then distribute one to me and one to herself; another to me and another to herself. I can almost hear God saying "eight plus for you; one for me. . . . " We'll stick with God's, "Plan A."

Thank you all for your love and for your concern,

—Stephen, Ginny, (Shaun, Anne and Elizabeth, Jaime, Jessica and?; Jesse, Jenni Joy and little Jessica Joy) Saint

Editor's Note: Did you notice the range of topics Steve and Ginny met head-on in this powerful chapter? Family solidarity, loyalty and love; parent-child relations; drugs, death & dying, clean living, missions and motivation, cross cultural relations, young love, teacher-pupil relations and a *faith that holds up in the test-tube of life!* Yes, all these vital subjects and more were courageously addressed in the true story you just read about a 20-year old youth who gave her world so *much* in a short life. I believe Peter Marshall was right: "It seems that God values a life by its donation rather than its duration."

Let me share a quote from p. 20 of *"THE GREAT OMISSION"* by Steve Saint: "Christ has commissioned us, His church, to distribute His offer of a *free remedy against the fatal sin disease that* has infected everyone, everywhere. The Christian church has been working at this for twenty centuries. We have done better in some of them than others. In the twentieth century we made a crucial mistake that debilitated what was otherwise a great effort. *We left most of the combatants out of the conflict!* That great omission hurt us." The rest of the book describes positive steps I-TEC, and all of us, can take to correct that "great omission." What world-changing ideas! Thanks Steve!

Why not order the book for your Pastor and church library? The address: I-TEC, 105 S.W. 147th Circle, Dunnellon, FL 34432. Price is $9.99 + S&H of $3.50 = $13.49.

It's my privilege to attend the Pleasant Grove United Methodist Church, Warsaw, IN, where Susannah (Saint) Barr, Steve's cousin, is our pianist. She introduced me to her family, including Stephen, who is the son of Nate Saint, one of the five young missionaries killed by the Waodani in Equador in 1956. My wife, Jodie and I had the joy of meeting her parents, Stephen and Gladys Saint, in November of 2002, at their home in Lansdale. And what a privilege! Here's an aged couple we believe are saints in more than name!

Thankfully,
J. Robert Boggs,—Editor

9

Providential Intervention

—CAROL HUFFER

After considering whether to tell my story openly, I finally decided that it is an opportunity to share one of the many instances where God *does* work in awesome ways *for* us. It's a fact: He is always *there for us.*

It was 1987, on a Thursday, before semester break began on Friday at Purdue University. My youngest son, a student there, was due home on Saturday, the day after break begins. It was the only day he could get a ride back to Warsaw.

My oldest son had moved to Ft. Wayne two years before, and I was totally *alone* for the first time in my life. My parents had both died many years before. I had gone through an emotionally devastating divorce not long before this day. My sister worked and lived overseas, and my brother lives in Idaho, and I had no close friends. I was really, all *alone,* so I felt—and the feeling ran deep. It's amazing how a man or woman, once divorced, can suddenly become aware that the friends you once *thought* were so close are now kind of "stand offish." Added to this "aloneness" I was not happy with my work. I just decided life was no longer worth living. I had gone through counseling sessions, and was told there were lots of people who loved and needed me, but I didn't see it that way at all.

That Thursday was absolutely the lowest day of my life. I decided to, "end it all." Commit suicide. Yes, me, the lady who now loves every minute of every day, regardless of what is happening around me! Not even Indiana's fast-changing weather bothers me. I'm *so grateful for every day!* But that wasn't the "me" then.

In the garage there were exposed rafters, and rope nearby. It was time to quit thinking about it and get it done. I knew people from work would come and check on me if I didn't show up for work the next day. A couple of them had expressed concern for me, (which was *caring* and *love* to which I deliberately closed my eyes.) That meant my son would *not* be the one to find me. My friends would come and find the body in the garage and save my youngest son that pain and trauma. As I stood in the garage deciding how to do all this, the telephone rang.

Now the boys and I had an unwritten rule in our house: no 'phone calls after 9:00 p.m. *unless* it's an emergency. I decided it must be one of the boys and there must be an emergency, so I went in and answered it. It was my youngest son asking me to leave the back door unlocked because he had finished his exams and had found a ride home from Purdue *yet that night!*

Wow! God intervened! He was, "right there for me!"

I went out and put the rope back where it had been and waited up for my son to come home. I told him the next day (after I sought professional and spiritual help) what had taken place. It messed up his break a bit because he was now afraid to leave me alone! But I was able to convince him that everything would be fine, and back to school he went.

I *knew* when I hung up the 'phone that Thursday night that *God* had worked in my life. This was no *"coincidence."* It was the *Good Lord,* and I knew what He was saying to me: *"You have things to do, lady! Now shape up!!"*

I did! And, Oh! The blessings He has given me! Far too many to list, but for a start: 1. True happiness. 2. Restored health. 3. Best of all, the sense *of being held in God's loving hands—always!*

I share with you this very, very personal part of my life because I was—and am—*sure* it was *God's* blessing on me! (Undeserved, yes, but *much appreciated.*) I have come to understand that God *never* gives us more of anything than we, by His grace, can handle. It is said so well in our "Instruction Manual." Maybe one verse might be helpful: "No temptation has seized you except what is common to man. And God is faithful; he will not let you be tempted beyond what you can bear. But when you are tempted, he will also provide a way out so that you can stand up under it." I Corinthians 10:13, (New International Version, by Zondervan).

Yes, I, who am normally a very "private" person, am sharing this with you because I believe, without doubt, that our caring God is with us and God is *for* us, every minute of every day, whether we know it or not. How comforting!

—Carol Huffer, 3/28/99

Editor's note: I have been a guest speaker at the large, active church where Carol sings in the choir. Dr. Frank Beard, her pastor, tells me that Carol is, indeed, a *"sparkling diamond"* in that suburban church and among all those who know her in the community. I'm glad to introduce this *real* and effective person to you via these pages.—JRB

10

It "Just Happened"?

—WESLEY EASH

I'm a retired Ohio business man. I consider myself
practical and "down to earth"—a "plodder" type—
trying to invest what time remains to me in worthwhile pursuits. That is why I joined the Gideons
years ago, taking Bibles and New testaments to
schools, hotel rooms, and prisons. When permitted or
invited, we give words of personal witness of what
God's Word has done in our own lives. We not only
buy the scriptures we give out, but we pay our own
way where we travel.

In 1980 a group of us loaded into a motor home
and were off to the big prison in Huntsville Texas on
just such a mission. We worked with the Bill Glass
Prison Ministry. After getting through the inspection
process on Friday, we ate in the cafeteria with the
prisoners. This experience signaled a change in my
own life as I shared the good news with prison
inmates. We assured them that God loves them *in
spite of all the wrong things they may have done in
the past.* Such sharing not only impacts my life, but
that of all our family.

I was sharing with an inmate how Christ had
changed my life for the better. Like many, he was not
paying attention as well as he might. Suddenly I
looked across the courtyard and said: "See that big tall

fellow over there? He weighs about 300 pounds. He's my son. And see that tall guy speaking to the group over to our left? He's my son too. The "good news" of God through Christ has changed our whole family. That's why we came all the way from up in Ohio with the good news that God can change your life too." He began to listen a lot more intently. Let me share with you just a few of our experiences to help you *listen up,* hopefully, a little better. Some of them may sound stranger than fiction to you, but they are true.

Like this one: A busload of us were on our way home from a witnessing and scripture distribution crusade when our driver stopped to pick up a hitch-hiker. I was on the front seat, alone. "Here!" I said. "You may sit with me if you like." He did, and after a while began to look at me so intently we were both almost embarrassed by it.

"Haven't I seen you somewhere before? Didn't you come to Huntsville, Texas, two years ago last November and talk with me about Jesus the Savior?"

"Yes! It *was* November" I said. "I thought I recognized *you too!* How are you doing?"

"Great!" he replied. "And guess what! I'm out of prison and been having a great time telling as many people as I can that Christ can set them free from their sins and get them ready for Heaven. Right now I'm on my way to Michigan. I have a brother there dying with cancer. I want to share with him that he can have the inner assurance he is forgiven, and will be in Heaven with the Savior when he dies. Forgiveness, new life, and the sure hope of life forever with Jesus—all just for the asking!"

Now tell me, was that a "happenstance" or was it a "providence" arranged by our loving God?

Instructions for prison visitors say *not to mention the word, 'Dad' to men in prison.* Far too many never had one, and if they did, he was the wrong kind. Doesn't that **shout** to us the importance of good vs bad parenting?. The bad costs society *billions* of dollars in taxes every year, besides all the more important— the non-financial costs. Instructors also urge you to be discreet in sharing your address/telephone number with prisoners. You could get a call or visit from someone with evil intent in years to come. One prisoner I talked to had killed ten people. There are all kinds, so caution is good.

I enter prisons trusting in God. I have many letters thus far with only good intent and results. All praise to our Lord! Let me tell you about a letter I got from an inmate a couple years ago. He had been sent to a 5-county prison only seven miles from my home. I remember him as a very large man with blue eyes. He attended our weekly Bible study. There was something about him I liked. After about six months here he was moved to a large prison. Three years later I received a letter from him. I knew instantly who it was from. He started with,

"Hi Brother Wes! I hope you remember me. I'm six feet and 320 lbs. I remember in your Bible study you had me lay hands with you on a fellow in a wheel chair. He decided that when he got out of prison he was going to find a way to witness to others about Jesus. He had my address for almost three years, and in his letter he said he had been out for six months, was active in church, and his pastor really 'preaches the Word.' He goes into a Senior Citizen's Home to share about Jesus."

He enclosed a check for $40, saying he wanted to sow to *my* ministry. He also sent his address and telephone number. I tried calling him, without success. Finally I wrote him, sending a check for $50. A week later I called again, and we had a long talk. I asked if he received my check, and he said, "Yes, and I sent a check for $50 to a fellow I had led to Jesus who is still in prison and will be out in a few weeks. (No clothes or money to start on.) But he wants to share the good news of Jesus when he gets out!"

So that's the way the gospel is spread—from person to person, inside prisons and outside. As someone said a long time ago: "It's like one beggar telling another beggar where to find bread!" It's still working—just like that! It's such fun! (JOY would be an even better word!)—Wesley Eash

P.S. A visit to the Eash's in Ohio might lead you to believe they are a, "prison ministry family." By being in five Prison Crusades you get a chrome-plated chunk of a old prison door in the shape of a Cross, with this inscription: *I was in prison and you visited me.* Wes & Mrs. Eash both have one. So does one son. One more Crusade and the other son will have one. They've ministered in OH, IN, IL, KY, MI, WI & GA, for a start. In case you ever wonder if there is lasting good done in prison ministries, take a look at Chuck Colson and Prison Fellowship. Thousands of converts all over the world! The Muslim religion is the fastest growing in the world. Two places it is growing fastest in America is College campuses & prisons. I pass along that last info. without comment, lest I get "foot in mouth" disease unnecessarily, like other "preachers" I've known.

—J. Robert Boggs, Editor

11

Faith Rests Where Reason Stalls

JOHN DAVID SCHAFFER

We have all had times when we had serious questions about God's presence, intentions, or even His existence. Such doubtful thoughts seem to assail our minds like hailstones—especially when life gets stormy, or when we have great personal stress. This is understandable. Although doubts about God's love and care for us may not demonstrate a lot of spiritual maturity, feeling like children abandoned by their parents when we need God most is close to a universal emotional reaction.

However, if we are willing to abandon those thoughts and shift our thinking, even the most devastating circumstances *can* open doors of growth opportunities and closeness to God we never dreamed possible when all was going to suit us. We can choose faith—to believe that God really *is* present and faithful to us—even hurting along with us. Trials can also develop courage to see and tackle new roles, jobs, and opportunities that will come our way because of a crisis. All these *will* come!

In difficult circumstances we need to understand that God did not cause the pain even though He allows it. (The concept of a God who is constantly intervening and the concept of mankind's "free will' are mutually exclusive!) Strange, is it not, that we seem willing to give up our human free will only when we are in trouble!

The Schaffer family learned a lot about the myriad ways God's grace abounds when our daughter, Heather! was in a terrible car accident. Heather! *chose* to officially spell her name with the exclamation mark punctuation, which is highly indicative of her view of life.

Following the accident—when we were completely *broken* and feeling *helpless*—we came to rely on the faith that God really *is* teamed up with us. Courage came to allow Him to work, along with the understanding that He did not *want* or *cause* this mishap. In reality, this most horrible event in our family history to date brought God from the lofty, abstract belief we previously held and put Him right down into our daily lives.

Life seemed good that day. It was an unseasonable February 10, 1993, with clear blue skies and a warm 68 degree temperature. My wife, Marcia, and I were enjoying the physical exercise and togetherness of splitting and stacking some firewood. As we waved good-bye to Heather! as she pulled out of our driveway to leave for work, we weren't giving much thought to God's presence in our lives. That would change in a mere two hours. Soon we were standing over her as she lay on a hospital gurney, unable to feel or move her legs. We wondered why we had this awful feeling that God had forgotten and abandoned us, especially in this, our time of dire need.

The surgeons said Heather!'s injuries were severe, permanent—with a "complete" spinal injury. She had taken a short "joy ride" down a country road on her way to work. Coming upon a hill with a 4-inch layer of winter road mix, she lost control of her sub-compact Toyota, flipping end-over-end 3½ times. Without her seatbelt fastened, and the collisions her

body had with the car's interior, it was a miracle that
Heather! was alive.

The months that followed were filled with grueling
physical therapy, adjustments to life in a wheelchair
and tremendous financial obligations. The accident dis-
located, compressed and *crushed* Heather!s 11th and
12th thoracic vertebrae. Her body was paralyzed from
that point down. The first time I watched her in early
therapy on a tilt table, I realized the impact such an
injury has on one's body. Raising her from a horizontal
position to a mere ten degree incline made her break
out in a profuse sweat and extreme nausea while she
begged the therapist to stop and return her to a flat
position. Her body had, indeed, received the shock of its
young life!

Marcia and I got so busy with trips to the hospitals and the mass of other details, we didn't have
time to feel sorry for ourselves. But I remember those
wee-hour "quiet moments." It's tough to feel alone,
vulnerable, like a failure as a father, husband, and
provider for one's family. In low moments like these
I tended to ask God *why* He would *allow* such a horrible thing to happen, especially to an innocent child
like Heather!

In those quiet, late and reflective times I would
ask God how He expected me to cope with this mess,
plus lead my family through the morass of difficult
things which were as yet unknown. Slowly I began to
see that He had *already* been preparing the way
through this major "disruption" by my change of jobs
and medical insurance. It was an insurance company
of which I had never heard. But they took an unusual
interest in helping us through it. Their "case manager" called us regularly, asking what *else* we needed,
and how *else* they could help! (Yes, I said it was an
insurance co. that took the *initiative*!)

My new job let me work nights, thus freeing my days to be at the hospital and offer support to my wife and family during my waking hours. Friends and members of our church family appeared at our door in a steady stream, bringing food, complete meals, cards and even money. People with tools and "know-how" helped with alterations in our house to make all areas accessible for Heather! when she would come home. One family even let us use their brand new car for those long trips to the rehab, hospital miles away. Our church set up an open account at a local gas station for us so that we would not have to worry about fuel money to visit Heather! One dear friend even started a "Help Heather!" fund at a local bank, publicized it, and did some fund-raising events. Money poured into the account, mostly from people we had never even heard of. (Pardon my moist eyes, folks, but how many places other than the U S A does this sort of "Christian" thing happen so often?)

Besides all this, the most impressive thing to the Schaffer family has been the presence, grace, love, and restorative compassion of our Heavenly Father that we have seen operative in our Heather! Rather than focusing on all that had been taken *from* her, in less than a day after her horrible accident we heard her remark to people that she had been, "Miracle-ized," referring to her surviving a wreck that could have so easily taken her life.

We, the family, have been amazed that this "attitude of gratitude" has tended to stick with Heather! throughout a tedious and painful rehabilitation, allowing her to attack the monumental therapy project with the zeal of a Heisman Trophy candidate! She worked hard, smiling and laughing when she did not feel like it, encouraging others—even the staff who worked with her so diligently.

No, Heather!'s outlook was not always this bright.
In fact, the reality of her new life as a paraplegic hit
home hard during her first few days in the rehab.
hospital. These were also my lowest moments, hearing my "little girl" voice her doubts about wanting to
live her life without walking; having to do everything
from a sitting position. But as we, her parents, family, friends, church family and many others in the
wider circle in the world *prayed* for her and for God's
gracious hand to stay upon her, we have *watched
Heather! change right before our eyes!* Her doubts
about wanting to live were replaced with a vivacious
zeal for life! Her fears about life with a disability
shifted to a confidence about being able to do anything she put her mind to. She seemed not to recognize her disability as a factor in her success, but she
made it one more challenge to try things in new and
creative ways. Would it surprise you to hear that in
a few years she was living just outside Los Angeles,
living alone, and working on her master's degree in
World Religions? Driving to classes all over the L A
area is a task many able-bodied people would find too
intimidating! But Heather!?

She does not view her disability as the defining
factor in her life/personality. There is practically no
activity she will not try. She goes camping, swims,
attends concerts and lectures and flies all over the
country. Nothing is alien to her that a little imagination and patience cannot help her meet head-on. It's
no wonder Heather! has become a heroine to many
people, touching them with her smile, attitude,
courage and her authentic love of life.

True, God has not healed Heather!'s spinal injury.
She is still paralyzed from her waist down; still uses
a wheelchair and hand controls on her car, and is still

dependent on accessibility to determine where she can and cannot go. Have we prayed for her full and complete recovery? Of course we have! Do God's answers to our prayers determine our attitude toward Him? No. I know He listens to our concerns. No shadow of doubt! Does God provide alternatives in our dilemmas? Always. Then *why* . . . ?

Ah h h! I was hoping you would ask that! Now listen to my answer at this stage of my comprehension and understanding: As of now, I believe that God's decisions about how to answer my prayers are His business, and it is my business to pray, to ask for Divine help and leading. The how, when and "in what ways" God answers is God's business and His alone. Furthermore, I also now understand that even if God were to *try* to explain His reasoning to me it would be a waste of time, because I could not even begin to comprehend it, given the great gulf fixed between my frail human mind and that of the Almighty, Omnipotent God-mind.

My confidence in God has grown to the point that even when certain specifics of my prayers are not met with immediate results that match my wants and subjectively perceived needs, God is *still listening, still caring, and still working* as our partner in all our difficulties. I know that I cannot conceive of God's total plan, of which our human lives are only a part. If I could understand it, I would have to be other than human. For now I am very happy with being just a human!

Meantime, it is enough for me to know that the Almighty, all-caring, all-knowing God lends His ear and full attention to every concern I bring to Him. I can rest in knowing that as long as I keep our lives, including Heather!'s, before Him, He will work *everything—every part of them*—out better than I could ever dream, hope, or imagine. (God said it through the apostle Paul, Romans 8:28, any version you name!) Here I rest my faith, and I have God's peace. I don't have to understand it!

—John David Schaffer

12

"Blended Family" Happiness

—Kathleen Alley

The signs were there-becoming self-absorbed, watching his diet, working out, sun bathing (now, this really was *strange!*), not attending church and becoming critical of me. But, unknowing and naive, I made excuses for him. "He's working so hard . . . away from home all week." I'll try harder.

Then, the 'phone call from "a friend" in his office—"Did you know your *husband and a secretary . . .*" Then came *my questions and his denials; my trust and his deceit.* Next, he "needed to be alone—he had personal problems to work out." Finally he moved out and moved in with a man from work (also getting a divorce.) He continued to call me. The children and I continued to trust and pray for him every day.

A mistaken call from a travel agent came concerning "your husband's and your trip to the islands." No more trust; no more denial—in its place a gut-wrenching pain; then anger, pity, withdrawal, even questioning God. Always "Why"? What did *I* do wrong? What can *I* do?

I thought I had been the ideal wife and mother. Though moving a lot with his jobs, we had worked together in church. He had been a deacon, and taught Sunday School. We led youth groups in three churches. I worked with the church women and taught Bible School. We loved our children dearly. We were diligent with home and family obligations.

Looking back on those bleak days when my world was falling apart, I can see the hand of God supporting me through family, friends, and my minister.

So many were so dear! What a marvelous *support group* God gave me through it all! I marvel at all the changes I went through in 18 months! There were special college courses I needed so that I could teach again and support the children and myself. There was the reduced *income* and *status* in society. Moving, dating again, single parenting. There are whole stories in each of these!

Divorce is acceptable when there is adultery, Jesus says. (St. Matthew 19:9). Though I knew that, it was still very hard to do. There were my children—precious and 8 year olds—what would we do? I would not hurt them for the world if I could help it, but . . .

Divorce has been likened to death. How true! It is. It's the death of a family God ordained it and as we know it should be! The grief process is the same—except more anger.

Ah, but God does not leave us helpless and alone! There is a life, "A. D." (after divorce.) In my case. God *eventually* sent me Howard . . .

Dating was not a priority with me, but I knew I had to do it—to "get out there." There were hilarious stories of some of my attempts, after eleven years of marriage, to jump-start my personal social life.

Howard was a co-worker of my mother's best friend. First there was the proverbial, "blind date." I almost didn't see him again after that. (He wrote a hilarious poem of our first date.) But I did see him again. Why? He was (and is) *so* good looking! Looks had never been a priority, (but it's a "positive" to fac-

tor in!) He has a beautiful voice. Being a speech therapist, I've always loved good voices. He knows more
jokes and *stories!* (I can't remember how to tell one
without writing it down!) He never meets a stranger.
Personality flows easily from him. Most important of
all, he was and is a *practicing Christian*—a wonderful man of God who knows the Bible and is *fun* to be
with. (Not a bad combination!)

It took me two years to realize God sent this wonderful person to *me!* I needed a "help meet," as the
Bible puts it, and so did he. He asked me to marry
him *before* we attended the play, *The Taming of the
Shrew.* "Better then than after," he said.

We became a *blended family*—with my becoming an
instant grandmother (via his married daughter) and
having a new 16-year old son to love. Howard became a
new "Dad" to my now 8 and 12 year olds. Would we suc-
cessfully and miraculously "pull this off"?

Answer? A definite "yes we *have,* for 21 years!"
What is the "secret" of the success? From the start
our sincere Christian faith has been the cornerstone
of our marriage and of our attempt at doing the
"humanly impossible"—*molding together a harmo-
nious and happy blended family!* Second, we deliberately put our past lives behind us. Howard and I
prayed sincerely for our former mates—even on our
wedding night. We *then* began to focus on each other
and our present family situation. We *asked* and then
trusted God to guide and bless *us* as we set out to
build a *dream home* on the ashes of two failures.

It worked! This is not to say there have not been
problems. Any Bible-reading Christian knows there
will always be obstacles in this sinful world. "We walk
by faith, not by sight" as it says in II Corinthians 5:7.
Thank God for a *lifting* word! We have found that our

positive, solid Christian faith allows God to lead us *through* any & all the problems of life. We find that our wonderful *living Lord* is so eager to do just that! We praise God daily for our family—our children—all four of them; our precious grandchildren, and our extended family all around us. God has been *so* good to us! The long-ago heartache has made me appreciate my wonderful husband and family even more than before. I have seen God working, "All things for good" in our lives and in many others. I think He must have said to me, "Kathy, *you can make it!*" And I say, "Thank You, Lord Jesus!"

—Kathy Alley, 1999

Editor's Note: Kathleen holds a Master's degree from Georgia State University in special education and keeps busy with her "special" students. Needless to say, with her personal qualities she always graduates a student with much *more* than just an expert "speech therapist" could possibly give. Those fortunate enough to have her for a teacher are truly, "special" people!

Howard is retired from the Lockheed-Martin Aircraft company where his major in engineering and art put him on the team that, several years ago, designed and built some of the world's biggest transport aircraft. Howard was always a very creative person, and this is still a part of him, even in retirement.

His new book is called *"Presumed Dead—A Civil War Mystery"* published by Bright Mtn. Books Inc. You'll want to get a copy of that interesting, historical book by Howard Alley soon!

Now read on . . .

Part II The Happy Marriage

—HOWARD E. ALLEY

What constitutes a happy marriage? Sociologists, psychologists and marriage counselors have wrestled with the question for generations. Yet the answer seems so uncomplicated and obvious to me that I wonder if it is *so* simple that the formula eludes the learned and is passed over by the masses of people who love for answers to sound profound? Let me invite you to look at four short words.

Love, honor, trust, respect.

Without all of these elements no marriage can be completely happy. Where there is no trust there is no respect. If respect is absent, there is no love. Without a steady flow of love, there is no honor. So you could say that these are four pillars that support every truly happy marriage. Many people make the sad mistake of thinking that wealth and material possessions bring happiness. Millions have tried that detour to the abiding joys of happy marriage, to invariably find themselves on dead-end streets. No, there is no substitute for love, honor, trust and respect.

Often you hear young people admonished: "If you want to have a happy marriage, you must really *work* at it!" That bothers me. Drudgery and happiness, to me, are two incompatible terms. If one must "knock himself out" by *forcing* himself to love, honor, trust and respect his mate, where lies the happiness? Happiness in marriage, as in every aspect of life, is grounded in a relaxed, free-flowing giving of ourselves to another individual, along with that person's gift of his/her life to us with true mutuality. It is not unlike a mountain spring from which the cool thirst-quenching water comes unbidden in a perpetual flow to refresh and sustain us. Or, to put it on a spiritual level—where certainly any successful marriage should be—this relationship between husband and wife can be compared to God's gift of salvation to mankind where we just accept it as a free gift. God does not expect us to work in his service to repay him for his gift of love, but rather we work to show our love for him and our appreciation for his gift.

Likewise, in marriage we give love and receive love as a natural manifestation of our mutual commitment to each other, with no strings attached. The work we do is not an installment payment on the love we receive, but an expression of our appreciation for that love.

I knew when I met her that Kathy was a "cut above the pack." Other women I had known—especially during my earlier college years—seemed shallow and superficial by comparison to Kathy. She came into my life with neither sham nor pretense. There was nothing phony about this gal. What you saw was what you got, and what I saw, I liked. She was petite, blue-eyed, and blond—and yes, I may as well admit it—sexy as a swim-suit model in *Sports Illustrated.* Yet, I soon learned she was a woman of uncompromising moral and spiritual values, compassionate, tender and caring. She was all woman, and proud of it. It is her belief that God created man and woman to fulfill different, but complementary roles in life. That is not to say that she sees woman as being subservient to man; for nowhere does God's plan suggest that; but it does establish man as the head of the family with the responsibility for its moral and spiritual leadership. Kathy subscribes to that concept and has always encouraged and supported me in that capacity.

Kathy and I did not fall madly in love "one enchanted evening when our eyes met across a crowded room," as the song says. Our relationship evolved gradually over a two-year courtship, during which time we experienced the joy and excitement of growing together, of sharing our values, our hopes and aspirations, our expectations of what we sought in a mate. We attended church services together, even prayed together before there was any discussion of an engagement.

And we played together: movies, concerts, plays and sports events, along with social events which stimulated our common desire for personal involvement with others In fact, that tendency in both of us toward personal involvement with strangers very nearly caused our relationship to end in disaster on our first date.

In an attempt to try to impress her that first night I took her to one of Atlanta's finest restaurants. We had just settled down at our elegant table in a secluded alcove surrounded by palms and fountains, when a loud-mouthed couple from out of town approached and asked if they could share our table, having arrived from another state without reservations at the restaurant. When they explained that they had come to Atlanta to celebrate their silver anniversary, I did not have the heart to refuse their appeal to join us, and sheepishly slid around to Kathy's side of the table to make room for the interlopers. Kathy and I were unable to exchange three words of conversation during the entire meal, while Huey enlightened us on the intricacies of managing his used car lot, and Flo related the exciting details of her hairdressing business back in their home town. I chomped on my steak while Kathy pushed her French food around her plate with her fork, and *fumed*.

As soon as etiquette would permit, we excused ourselves from the table and escaped to the lounge for a brief
dance, after which Kathy demanded through clinched
teeth that I take her home, since I had ruined—as she
put it—our first and *only* date. Well, we had words on the
way home, as the old folks used to say, but I didn't get to
use mine! In time, Kathy cooled down, though, and
allowed me to come back on a probationary basis, and I
gradually worked my way back into her good graces.

As the months went by and we became more
involved with each other, one of our goals was our
mutual desire to earn the respect and acceptance of
our children from previous marriages; her two
younger ones, Rusty and Shannon, and my sixteen-
year old son, Matt, and married daughter, Jennifer.
When Kathy and I eventually married it was not the
first for either of us. Both had experienced the
heartache and devastation of broken marriages,
especially the impact it had on the children. Neither
of us had desired divorce, having been brought up
believing that marriage vows are for life; yet each of
us accepted our share of responsibility for the
breakup. But we both felt that our previous failures
could serve to make us stronger and more fully committed partner in our future marriage to each other.
In a sense, the human will is like a piece of metal
which draws its strength from being subjected to
intense heat. Any structural engineer knows that a
steel beam cannot be used in the construction of a
bridge or high-rise building until it has been heat-
treated to solidify and harden its molecular struc-
ture, thereby insuring its strength and integrity. So
it is with the human experience. We become stronger
and more capable of coping with the pressures and
adversities of everyday life after having passed
through the heat of the blast furnace.

From the beginning of our serious courtship Kathy and I sought to identify and resolve some of the doubts and suspicions which inevitably confront every couple contemplating marriage. We freely discussed our positions on money matters, religion, child discipline, in-law relationships and our personal expectations of what each of us would bring to our union. We recognized that these considerations can be very detrimental, if not totally destructive, if not resolved *before* the marriage.

And let me hasten to say this concerning sex, because it plays such an important part in a successful marriage, yet is treated with such reckless abandon by our current society. During our courtship Kathy and I mutually agreed to refrain from letting the bedroom be the experimental laboratory in determining how well suited we were for marriage! We embraced a philosophy that said, "If the feeling is not right above the belt, it won't be right below the belt." That statement, by the way, wouldn't be a bad slogan for today's young people. In other words, sex without love is as unfulfilling as marriage without commitment.

When we set our wedding date it was with a good deal of confidence that our decision would meet with God's approval; for we knew there were a number of circumstances which we would find most difficult without His guidance and intervention. First, we each faced the ordeal of having to sell the present home in which we lived in order to satisfy the terms of our divorces. Secondly, since we lived in different counties, we had to reach an agreement as to where we would locate our new family, hopefully in an area which would have the least adverse impact on the children's school activities. Before this became an issue, however, Kathy, in her generous, unselfish way, recognized that my son Matt, who was older than Rusty and Shannon, and deeply engaged in sports and academics in his high school would be much more adversely affected by a major change than would be her younger children. So she graciously volunteered to leave the familiar surroundings of her own county and relocate in my home town. For this, both Matt and I were very grateful.

God led us to the perfect house in which to merge our two families: a big rambling place, spacious, but not elegant. Unfortunately, though, it was listed at a price far beyond our budget, and we dismissed it as unattainable. Then a strange thing happened: a representative from the bank that owned the property called and offered to discount the price, but still we could not afford it. He called back again, then again, each time reducing the price. Still we hesitated. At last he called and asked us to make an offer. To myself I asked God if *He* was trying to put us in this house. He said, "Yes, go ahead and bid." I blurted out a price 20% under the asking price. The banker said, "Sold!"

Still leery, I hired a professional engineer to come in and check out all the features of the house, halfway suspecting it contained some drastic defect. The engineer gave it a clean bill of health, and we signed on the dotted line. (We are still there after twenty-one years of joyous living!)

Kathy, meanwhile, after her divorce, had returned to college where she got her master's degree in education in order to resume her teaching career. God led her to a teaching job in a fine school not far from our new home. Here she was able to enroll Rusty and Shannon, thereby making it possible for the three of them to travel to and from school together, and more importantly, to enable Kathy to be close to the children during the school day.

A number of other decisions and considerations had to be met during this awesome transition period (ten in all) but in every case God helped us solve the problems, opened doors of opportunity where needed, and guided/led our careful plans in good and right paths as we trusted His divine purposes for our lives.

The children have long since grown up and gone from our home, but not from our hearts. We hear from one or two of them almost daily, and the bonds which made us a family are even stronger now than when we began.

Kathy has far exceeded everything I ever dreamed of in a wife. She is respected and admired by all who know her. She is really idolized by countless handicapped students to whom she has given hope and the promise of a successful life. She has always looked upon her role in the lives of these troubled youth as a ministry, and not just an occupation.

Have we had a happy marriage all through these years? Yes, indeed! Has it always been easy? Certainly not. Can anyone have a happy marriage after a first failure? Yes, we believe most anyone can. But don't try it unless your faith is fast anchored in God, first of all. Then be sure you have a solid trust in each other that you are confident *will* withstand some storms.

Above all, never forget the four basic elements of your commitment: *Love, honor, trust, and respect.* Love your mate because you respect them; respect them because you trust them; and honor them because you love them.

I love my Kathy because she is easy to love. To know her and *not* love her would be almost impossible! I'd have to really *work* at that!

Here's my, *ODE TO KATHLEEN* I gave her on our fifteenth anniversary.

A candlestick of gladness stood unlighted, ashen, cold
Upon the cheerless mantelpiece of my remorseful soul.

I knew not of its presence; lost, it stood within the gloom,
Behind the shaded windows of my solitary room.

Unheard, some gentle stranger raised my latch and
crept within,
To light my waxen taper and restore the warmth again.

A melted drop seeped downward into aspirations old
Discarded on the hearthstone of my bleak and lonely soul.

A flick'ring flame leaped upward to bring light where
shadows dwelt,
And I saw her there beside me in the happiness I felt.

Then, hand in hand we ventured on a new and lovelier
clime,
Inward glowing, somehow knowing we had found a
place sublime.

Through the years the flame she kindled burns within
my heart serene,
And I know with calm assurance, I will always love
Kathleen.

—Howard E. Alley

My First Date with Kathy
(Poem based on a true story)
—Howard E. Alley

Our mutual friend, Dot Moody, introduced Kathy
and me. The intro led to our first date on March 19,
1976. Wanting to impress Kathy, I took her to the
beautiful Ambassador restaurant in Atlanta and

ordered the finest cuisine on the menu. No sooner had we started dining and getting acquainted than up walked a strange couple and asked to join us. They explained that they had come all the way from Spartanburg, S.C., to celebrate their 25th wedding anniversary but had not made reservations. Since the place was crowded, and it was their anniversary, I didn't have the heart to refuse them. I invited them to sit down, though it almost cost me my future with Kathy.

THE POEM

"Call her quick!" Dot Moody urged me,
"Call her now while there's still time,
When the word gets out she's dating,
You'll be left way back in line."

"Well," I said, "If she is willing
To go out with someone older,
I will give her 'phone a jingle
When I feel a little bolder."

"Don't wait, man!" Dot warned emphatic
"Make your move. I kid you not,
Better get your tail in motion;
Strike now while the iron is hot.!"

"Oh, relax," I answered, smiling,
"Have you stopped to think of this?
It's not likely that a boyfriend's
Very high upon her list.

"Especially since you chose to tell me
She just dumped that other clown,
It would seem a wee bit foolish
For someone else to come messing 'round."

"Well, I've warned you," Dot said sternly,
"Don't blame me if you lose out;
If you had an ounce of gumption
You'd already have asked her out."

Well, I called her Tuesday morning
And I said, "Hey, look, Kathleen,
"Would you care to join me Friday
For some really fine cuisine?"

"Sure," she said, all soft and silky,
"I would like that very much.
But I want it understood, though,
I prefer that we go Dutch."

"Okay, sure," I said, not eager
To split up the dinner check,
"Time was I'd have been insulted ,
But times have changed, so what the heck.

"You pay your tab; I'll pay mine,
Then no one's obligated
To hold on to our relation
If we feel the bloom has faded."

I showed up at eight, precisely,
Wearing my new leisure suit,
When I saw her in the doorway,
"Wow!" I said, "but aren't you cute."

She smiled sweet and thanked me kindly,
Saying, "You're not bad yourself."
This encouraged me so greatly
Tried to kiss her as we left.

"Hold it, Bub, you're bad mistaken,
If you think I'm some dumb bimbo,
Keep that up and you'll awaken
In a state of utter limbo!"

"Sorry, you looked so delicious,
I misread your private wishes.
Let's go out and try some dishes,
Later we'll discuss the kisses.

We set out in my green Chevy
As the setting sun went down,
Wound up in a swanky restaurant
In the better part of town.

Palms and fountains all around us
Cast a soft romantic spell.
In a while it seemed for certain
We would hit it off quite well.

We had steaks with all the trimmings,
Served with rare imported wine,
Seated in a nook secluded
From the throngs who came to dine.

Just as we began our eating,
Making easy conversation
We were rudely interrupted
To our utter consternation.

Up walked Florence and loud-mouth Huey,
Greeting us like lost relations.
"Could we share your table, neighbors?
We don't have no reservations.

"We drove in from South Care-lina;
It's our silver anniversary.
Used to come here in the fifties,
Didn't need no reservation."

"Well, I guess so," I said meekly,
Sliding round beside my date.
They flopped down and started talking,
Elbows almost in our plate.

"Flo, here, runs a beauty parlor
South of Spartanburg, you know;
I'm in sales. Hardware and Plumbing,
Never saw sales quite so slow."

Then they ordered from the menu
Almost everything it featured.
When it came the two consumed it
Like a pair of jungle creatures.

Appetizers, soups and salads,
Smacking lips and flying hands,
Conversation growing louder
When the boys struck up the band.

Kathy cowered in her corner,
I sat stupefied and dumb;
Flo and Huey beating cadence
On our table like a drum.

Leaning close to Kat I shouted,
"Wanna dance?" She nodded yes.
Waving bye to Flo and Huey
We made haste to flee their mess.

On the dance floor, Kathy sizzled,
"Just forget it, it's too late
I can't b'lieve you let those turkeys
Ruin our first and only date!"

"Hold it, dear," I said, defensive,
"Let's consider this a bit:
On our Silver Anniversary
We may need a place to sit."

"Pooh," she said, "don't get presumptuous
Counting chickens 'fore they hatch.
We don't even know each other,
Little chance we'd make a match!"

"Fine!" I said with wounded ego,
"Here's your portion of the check!"
"The heck you say! You ruined our dinner
Don't ask me to split no check!"

Well, that first date was a failure,
Losing her distressed me much . . .
Then I thought of what she'd told me:
She preferred to go it Dutch!

Twenty years now we've been married;
Early on we struck a deal:
I agreed to do the loafing,
While she works on to pay the bills!

13

Horrendous Toys!

—Cynthia Brown-White*

"Come here, Cindy! I have a new toy for you to play with." This is a memory of when I was a little girl three or four years old. A man, I assume a neighbor, was sitting on our back step. His pants were open and he was exposing himself. I do not remember what I thought, but he wanted me to touch him and I couldn't understand. He said it was a "new game" to play. I have no idea how many times this happened— but I remember just where he was sitting on the step. He told me not to tell; it was "a secret."

Another neighbor I remember was a boy of 12 or 13 who, many times, took me to the granary where he exposed himself, too. I have shut these instances from my memory, except for the dirt floor, mud daubers on the wall, the many eerie cobwebs and *dirt* everywhere! (Not to mention the dirt that was in the kid's mind!) Again, I was told not to tell, as something *bad* would happen if I did.

As I grew, a little older cousin who liked to play hide-and-go-seek with us younger children seemed to prefer hiding with us girls. I don't know what he did to the other girls, but he liked to touch me in private

---

*Not her real name.

areas. Again, he would threaten to tell if I said any-thing. Thus, even before puberty, I began to think that all boys and men did this, and I tended to avoid them.

A few years later, my sister married and her new husband liked to tease me. I would fight back when he began to explore my body. If he found me in a room by himself, he would push me up against himself. Later he began to expose himself to me. No matter how I tried to avoid him, he seemed to find me alone. He raped me on several occasions.

Now I began to feel that something was wrong with *me;* that I was dirty and no good. It seemed to me that *all* men wanted to touch in the wrong places; *so it must be my fault!*

The first big step in my *deliverance* from this steadily growing *horror* was in church when I was twelve years of age. The preacher gave the invitation for those who wanted to be forgiven for their sins and become "saved" to come forward to the altar of prayer. I wanted to go forward, but I felt that I was unfor-givable. In spite of this terrible feeling of unworthi-ness, I gathered my courage and went forward. Soon I was surrounded by loving people who sincerely prayed for me. My faith took hold of God's love that I felt reaching out to me, and I "believed" God's word that He would save me. That was only a first step, but for me it was a *big* one.

As might be expected, Satan seemed to know my weak points in feeling so terrible and so unworthy. That furthered my idea that all men had this terri-ble flaw of sexual promiscuity. Any relationship I had with the opposite sex, I either "stayed my distance" or I purposely tempted them to see if they would take advantage of me as others had in the past. This did nothing to help my feeling of being "dirty," as it was thought of at that time.

Again I went forward in church and asked God to forgive me. This time my understanding and maturity had developed enough for me to experience a real "change of heart and life." I thought the way out of my problems was to ask God to sanctify (cleanse) my heart. For this I prayed, and I know God was eager to do just that. Someone pointed me to I John 1:9, and the words "forgive and cleanse."

Now I understand why so many who have abusive fathers and have been lustfully used sexually find it hard to love their Heavenly Father. The name "father" to those who have been victimized by some man or by a human father would certainly not have the same meaning as to those with a godly dad.

In God's grace and providence I finally met a young man who later became my husband. He discouraged *any* slight "advances" I made toward him. Wow! At last a, "different breed" of a man! *Good* I thought. He was truly different, and I finally was able to fall in love with him and say, "Yes!" when he asked me to marry him.

I am so thankful for this man! God has given us a good relationship that has helped to untwist my warped view of men. Now think of that, men! God used *one good man* to help undo the evil and grief that for many years several other men had brought on me! My husband is a sincere Christian. But even good men need to be watchful and "set a guard" *if* sex sin is a weakness with them. Don't be afraid to ask your wife to forgive you when you need it! Let her help to "pray you through" your weak times. We need each other! Pride is a mortal enemy to both sexes!

Another aspect of my wounds is theological. Does Jesus love us for sex? He, being masculine and my experiences of early childhood gave the Tempter room to try to manipulate and poison my thoughts. I sometimes wondered if I could ever have a close relationship with Jesus. My mind said that sex had nothing to do with the love of God, but the doubts invaded my mind anyway. I knew that Jesus was without sin of any kind while He lived on earth. Yet, to wholeheartedly accept the love of Jesus was a long, long struggle for me. Over and over the thought crept in that men like sex. *Satan seems to know just where our weak points are,* and mine was the frequent return of such thoughts. The result was that I did not have the yearning to be alone with Jesus that so many people talk about. Fear replaced that yearning. I began to be afraid that I might blaspheme against the Holy Spirit!

When overwhelmed by these questions and doubts, I have been amazed at God's patience and love. Often our Lord Jesus has assured me, like "Doubting Thomas" that He loves me and died in my place; that He is, indeed, my Savior and Lord. He said, "Just talk to *me* when these doubts come to your mind."

This I have done for many months and years now. Peace, that only God could give, has been mine. I have been greatly helped by a quote from Dr. David Seamand's book. *Healing of Damaged Emotions,* page 56: "Are you in that picture? Freed, forgiven, a son, a daughter of God, a member of His family, but thinking of yourself as a worm or a grasshopper? Low self-esteem is Satan's deadliest psychological weapon, and it can keep you marching around in vicious circles of fear and uselessness."

Dr. Seamands continues as he quotes from I John 3:1-2 (J. B. Phillips translation): "Consider the incredible love that the Father has shown us in allowing us to be called 'children of God'—and that is not just what we are called, but what we are. Our heredity on the God-ward side is no mere figure of speech—which explains why the world will no more recognize us than it recognized Christ. Oh, dear children of mine (forgive the affection of an old man), have you realized it?

"Here and now we are God's children. We don't know what we shall become in the future. We only know that, if reality were to break through, we should reflect His likeness, for we should see Him as He really is."

I am growing in learning how to deal with all this "garbage" of my past. Recently, I heard someone say, "Let the past be the past and don't get bogged down and 'stuck' there! Move on in the *Sonlight* of God's love and press forward and upward toward our Heavenly hope in Christ Jesus."

Be assured that I *could have* allowed my most unfortunate early experiences with males to turn me bitter against life, God, and all things worthwhile. I could have "played the blame game" that seems so popular in society today. I could have easily become a raving, angry feminist. At a very young age I knew I had the awesome power of choice given by a benevolent Creator. I used that power.

I deliberately used God's gift and chose to look up and seek the way *through* the unwanted dirt that surrounded me in what should have been a sweet, innocent childhood. I found the way *through* and *over* it. Later, in the Lord's timing, I found a wonderful husband. Together God gave us a beautiful family of which we are very proud. It seems like a big bonus that He also gave us a host of friends far and wide. For all these rich gifts I am most *grateful* and say, "Thank you, Lord Jesus!

I also have used my power of choice to share these painful memories for the very first time (rather late in life) to:

1. To assure you who have been violated that you do not have to let *anything* keep you from being the "whole" person our Lord intended.
2. To offer parents "helpful hints" in rearing *your* precious children.
3. To try to "leave a marked trail" upward through the morass to joy at last!

14

"The Lighter Side" or "Just For Fun"

Even in a book with serious purpose, some pages of humor are in place. Shirley Wyse is an artist who paints beautifully with oil paints. In this chapter she uses her talent to paint word pictures. Remember back when we were criticizing Communist Russia for their idolatry of materialism? Facetiously, Shirley could be aiming the same criticism at our American "materialism"!

Let's give it careful attention! She did this "fun" thing for "Seniors." But the message is also *powerful* for us all! Thanks, Shirley!—J. Robert Boggs, Editor

The Bag Lady

—SHIRLEY WYSE

You probably wonder why I live in the streets. Well, I chose to. I had a nice house, nice clothes, a car, a garden, plenty of food and lots of gadgets and appliances-all the things we think we just have to have. In other words—I had lots of stuff. Real "STUFF!"

As I began to realize I was getting older, I said to myself, "I'm getting tired of trying to "keep up with the Joneses"—you know, collecting more and more stuff, cooking, cleaning—you name it.

I hate cooking and I'm terrible at it, too. I figured out some ways to disguise my cooking deficiencies. When I had company I'd serve scalding hot coffee first. They'd burn their tongues and couldn't taste the food. When I'd serve gravy I'd ask: "One lump or two?"

Back home up north, I lived on what I called, "Clean Street." (Kinda' like some streets here in our mobile park.) I had some neighbors that were so clean that the snow in their yards even seemed whiter than mine. (Really, I think she must have bleached it every night.) She even scrubbed her driveway e-v-e-r-y day! (I scrubbed mine once—I think it was back in 1972.)

One morning I woke up and heard a, "Swish, swish." So I looked out my door and hollered: "There's a fly speck two inches left of the steps" and she told me to "SHUT UP!" I couldn't understand why.

Well, I hate to clean. My oven once got so crusty I could only bake one cupcake at a time! I didn't want my neighbors to know I hated cleaning, so I got two sets of throw rugs. I shook the new one out the front door in the daytime and the others out the back door at night. My husband refused to eat raisin bread after we found a rat in the kitchen.

Twice a year I open the living room drapes, put a stepladder at the picture window with a bucket and rag on it so the neighbors will think I'm cleaning.

And keeping houseplants? Forget it! The only green and growing thing in my house was mold growing in the refrigerator.

I got so worn out trying to keep up with everyone that I looked older and wrinklier than all my friends.

They were all getting cosmetic surgery (that costs a fortune) and the results weren't too good either. One had silicone implants and they slipped down. One had hip reduction surgery and the swelling never went down. Another had a face lift. The doctor dropped it in-stead. She had it done over so many times that now, every time she smiles, her leg raises. So I decided to rule out all that surgery stuff.

But while I was talking to my doctor during the examination, he used some medical terms I didn't understand. So I remembered this medical book of terms a mountain friend of mine gave me. Definitions like: Outpatient = "one who has fainted." Varicose veins = veins that are very close together. Protein = those in favor of teenagers. Medical staff = a Doctor's cane. Morbid = a higher offer. Secretion = Hiding something. Nitrate = lower than the day rate. Artery = The study of fine paintings. Minor operation = Coal digging. Caesarian section = A district in Rome. Fester = Quicker. Tumor = An extra pair. Congenital – Friendly. Urine – Opposite of "you're out." I sure learned a lot about medical terms from that hill dictionary when I got home. Next time I think I'll take the little book with me to the doctor's office and educate him a bit.

And speaking of "stuff", I start every fall to sort out my stuff in hopes of getting rid of some of it. What kind of stuff? Well, there is closet stuff, drawer stuff, attic stuff, and basement stuff. I separate the good stuff from the bad stuff, then I stuff the bad stuff anywhere the other stuff is not too crowded—until I decide if I will ever need any of the bad stuff.

When the Lord calls me home, my children may want the good stuff but will probably stuff the bad stuff in bags and take it to the dump where all the other stuff that people didn't want has been taken.

When we have company they bring bags of stuff with them. When I visit my son, he always moves his stuff so I will have a little room for my stuff. My daughter-in-law always clears a drawer of her stuff so I will have room for my stuff. Why wouldn't it be easier just to leave my stuff at home and use their stuff?

This fall I had an extra closet built so I would have a place for all the stuff too good to throw away but not good enough to keep with my best stuff. Maybe you don't have this problem, but I seem to spend a lot of time and thought on sorting and keeping different kinds of stuff. There's food stuff, cleaning stuff, medicine stuff, clothes stuff, and even outside stuff. How much simpler life would be if we didn't have all this stuff!

There is stuff we use to make us smell better than we usually smell. There's stuff to make what hair we have look better . . . Stuff to make us look younger; stuff to make us look healthier; stuff to hold us in and stuff to fill us out. There's stuff to read, stuff to play with, or entertain us and stuff to eat until we are stuffed. Our lives are filled with stuff: good stuff, bad stuff, little stuff, BIG stuff, useful stuff, and junk stuff. Everybody has stuff.

And you know what? One day we'll lie down and die & leave all this stuff. If we go to Heaven, we'll not need *any* of this stuff. And if we don't . . . all the stuff in the whole world won't do us a speck of good, or stop our grief for wrong choices.

Are You "Over the Hill?"

You can find out, for sure, by taking this test and scoring yourself! You are "Over The Hill" when . . .

_____ you feel like the "morning after" and you haven't been anywhere.

_____ your back goes out more than you do.

_____ you have given up all your bad habits and you still don't feel good.

_____ you have joined a health club and you're too tired to get there.

_____ you are taking your "one a day" vitamins three times a day.

_____ the gleam in your eye is the sun hitting your tri-focals.

_____ the Boy Scouts volunteer to help you cross the street.

_____ "rigorous exercise" means giving up the remote control for a while.

_____ you consider "Sex Drive" the name of a street.

_____ the "morning after" usually lasts all day.

_____ "life in the fast lane" refers to the grocery express check-out.

_____ you stop to think and forget to start again.

_____ you have stopped "feeling your oats" and started feeling your corns.

_____ caution is the only thing you exercise.

_____ the candles on your cake cost more than the cake.

_____ you get winded playing cards.

_____ your knees buckle but your belt doesn't.

_____ if you can remember when the air was clean and sex considered dirty.

_____ everything has started to wear out, fall out, or spread out.

_____ you have received a birthday card from that guy on TV.

_____ you have been contacted by the Guiness Book of World Records

_____ Bingo is becoming your favorite "contact sport."

_____ Large black birds sail in circles fly in low circles over your head.

If you checked 0–10, you're lying . . . 16–20, you may be having a mid-life crisis . . . 21–25, you are fading fast. 26–30, you need to check your will.

15

"So You Wanta' Be a Detective?

(Like Sgt. Vince Andolina)

—J. ROBERT BOGGS

When I was growing up life was an exciting adventure. I wanted to go places and do things. I like to remember fascinating people and interesting events, with the emphasis on *people*. It is people who give events and things their meaning.

Remember when you were a little girl or boy? People would ask, "What do you wanta' be when you grow up?" Some of us had more than one thing we wanted to be . . . a dozen maybe! I wanted to be an engineer to run a powerful locomotive that pulled a train. Later I wanted to pilot an airplane. Still later I wanted to teach agriculture and help young farmers re-build the thin Georgia topsoil. Finally I wanted to be a doctor to help sick people regain their health. Those were only a few of the things I wanted to do at one time or another.

How many of you ever wanted to be a great detective and unravel "whodunits"? That is only one of the many things I never got to do. All of us finally learned that life is too short to do all the interesting and exciting things we wanted to do.

I did have the privilege of knowing a retired C I A agent. He traveled the world, made lots of money, and had about every "high adventure" one could imagine.

The only bad thing about knowing him is (you guessed it) I can't share much of what I know.

Fortunately, I do have another detective friend who retired years ago from the Buffalo N.Y.P.D. He told me a story he said I could share with anyone, so here goes:

One day three men knocked at the door of an 80-year old lady who lived alone. They were dressed as gas-meter readers, complete with hard hats. She let them in. Soon she saw her mistake. They took turns raping her, beat her up, bound and gagged her, then took her money and jewelry and left. They hit her in the face so hard it broke her denture in two pieces, to say nothing of the swollen black eyes and cut lips. The watch they took was the one she got after serving her company 50 years.

She lay there for eight hours in her blood, urine and defecation before neighbors/family came and found her. But she was still alive! Detective Sgt. Vince Andolina was on the investigative team from the Buffalo Police Department assigned to the bloody case. First they visited the hardware stores to check their memory of recent purchases of rope. At the fourth one the manager remembered three men buying rope, and what they looked like, and said one they called, "Cookie." That was a start.

Now for the pawn shops. At one they found the watch, engraved with her name. And he had the address of the guy who pawned it!

He was arrested. With a little "persuasion" he remembered the other two and they were arrested. In the trunk of their car was found more rope and duct tape. With the woman's positive identification, the three men were charged, tried and put in prison for five years. We hope in jail their "hearts" changed.

Vincent shared with me that the 80-year-old lady was so grateful to him and the Buffalo P.D. that she kept in contact and became a good friend to him and his wife. The last time he saw her she was 98 years old. He says that bit of police work was not only successful, but "the memory of it has brought me deep inner satisfaction for all these years."

My thanks to Det. Sgt. Vincent Andolina of the Buffalo N.Y.P.D!

And we thank God that he survived those years of service in a "high risk" job and can now enjoy family and friends in a much lower risk environment down in sunny Florida! Let us be faithful to pray for all our law enforcement officers, firemen and other public servants! Etched indelibly on memories of us Americans is what happened on 9/11/2001 in New York City and the real heroism of the men and women on the Police and Fire Departments. We have heard and/read many of the stories. Many are known only to God. They will never be told, but God remembers!

The danger for us is that we tend to forget, or push memories of bad things onto the "back burner" and for all practical purposes, forget. We quit expressing our gratitude as we should. We all have a debt that we can never pay as long as we live. These to whom we owe it do not expect payment. But it is not too much to expect that we maintain "an attitude of gratitude" toward our friends like Vincent Andolina and say a heart-felt "Thanks" occasionally.

Speaking of gratitude, some of us are still alive who have vivid memories of the horrors of World War II, and the literal hell-on-earth created by one Adolph Hitler and the Nazi Party (those who allowed themselves to be sucked into the cesspool in which he and they drowned.) Who but God can calculate the cost in lives/money of that war! I hope you will never forget the tragic stories told by Francis Trotter,

Wm. Mercer Massengale and Raimer Schultze related in this book. As Trotter said, "These terrible stories have not been told to glorify war in any way, but to let us know the great debt we owe those who died for us and our freedom!"

16

Surprise Joys and Blessings

—JUDY OSBORNE

Tears rolled down my face as I tried to process what I had just heard. My husband of 17-1/2 years wanted a divorce! We had our share of problems, like all married couples, but he never wanted to discuss them. When communication goes, just about everything else goes with it.

I choked back the tears, and was finally calm enough to ask the dreaded question women fear: "Is there someone else?" He looked at the kitchen table silently for a long time and finally answered, "No." (He couldn't look me in the face or make eye contact.)

I was naive enough to believe him. A week later when I related this to my attorney she nearly bent double with laughter, but later she cried with me.

I was 29 when I married him. His wife had died of cancer only a year and a half before. I was much too young to assume the responsibility of three children besides my one. But marriage to me was not something to *try*. It was a for-life commitment, "for better or worse . . ." I thanked God often that the children were good ones, and with a committed partner I could have handled the assignment. But now . . .

The next twelve months were chaotic, to say the least. Mother and Dad celebrated their 50th wedding anniversary. When planning the celebration we weren't sure if her cancer would allow her to have the strength to go through with it. But the party was beautiful, and so was she. She died six months later. My mother was a young-looking woman—beautiful outside and inside! I still miss her every day, and still have urges to call her . . . Unlike most women, she had no time for idle chatter or gossip, or time for hours on the 'phone, but always had time for kind, positive, meaningful conversation. She was often in the kitchen cooking food to take to someone ill. That was my "truly Christian" mother! I grew up looking over her shoulder as she read her Bible.

I didn't think much of it at the time because I was young. Now I realize how blessed I was to have a mother like her. She stayed home with us three when other mothers opted to "farm out" their greatest treasure, their children, to someone—anyone—so they could bring more money for the family budget. Mom and Dad had their priorities right, and they were blessed. So were we, their three children. We lived across the street from a good church. We attended regularly. My uncle Bob said, "Judy, how does it feel to have an "angel" for a mother and live across the street a good church?" I took it for granted then, but now I realize that *God has blessed me greatly!*

During the divorce process and all that entailed I had to find a place to live and find a job that would support me. I had never lived alone, and I gave up my career to marry him and be at home for the children. Divorce, Mother's "homegoing," and a new career were all new to me—and all in one year! How could I make it? By God's grace and help from many of His people!

It was a year of "discoveries" for me. I had been a member of Mt. Carmel Christian Church in Stone Mountain, Georgia, for thirty years. My Bible Class, the "Christian Workers" (another blessing I had taken for granted, not realizing they were among the greatest people on earth) came to my rescue! The teacher, Patty Ward, said they had a basement apartment I could live in as long as I needed to. I hung up the 'phone and broke into tears. Soon another member. Bob Crutchfield, found a nice condo I could afford—two stories with no yard to keep! My sister, Carol Hope, is a high school computer teacher, but the only thing I could do extremely well was type. I had been a secretary and didn't want to do that again, but do it again I would if I needed to.

About this time a medical transcription company called *Transquick* in Atlanta sent out representatives to high schools for "career day" to recruit transcriptionists. Legal transcription was my field, but they gave me a chance to learn the medical. After two weeks of stressful training, they said I would never make it. But the trainer's assistant, Cindy, pled my case and they gave me another chance. (I had a lot on my mind right then.) After eleven years I'm still working for them! I will remember Cindy and thank God for that opportunity. Making a good living and working at home many people would like to do. What a deal! *God has blessed me!*

About a year after Mom died my Dad met this lovely Christian lady, Marie, and they decided to get married. Her husband of 53 years had passed away, and it was great for both of them and we were all happy. Dad said, "Marie is a Christian and a real lady, and there aren't too many of those available any more." We all shed tears *of joy* for them at the wedding. I had been a step-mother before, and knew the role was not easy. But this Marie is great—so easy to love! She even has a good sense of humor. Again, *God has blessed me!* And I'm getting less "surprised" all along. God is good, all the time!

Dad's re-marrying changed all our lives for the better. We're all happy for him. Marie is as good as they come. But little did I realize that this new stepmother had a nephew. Bill, she and his mom wanted me to meet. (Just to see if perchance we "hit it off" together.) Well, I was enjoying being single, and doing well financially. But we did have that "first date."

I knew Bill came from a good Christian family (who were Southern Baptists). And I came to know him as a dedicated Christian gentleman. But I was (shall I say *surprised?*) to find, after a brief courtship, that he was understanding, sweet, compassionate, and . . . you name it! All I could wish or ask for, and more.

Bill and I were married July 2, 1996, during the Olympics in Atlanta. We were, "living happily ever after" for quite a while before I discovered Bill wasn't perfect. But even sooner, he found out that I was not perfect! Now what?

I'm glad you asked, because I want to tell you. I discovered that I could safely talk with this sweet, understanding husband of mine about any problem I have. Often we come up with a better solution after sharing than either of us had at the start! Which leads me to say: *If a married couple cannot (or will not) communicate, you have a stumbling block that is almost insurmountable.* But if you are willing to calmly, loving, talk things out you will be surprised by the *JOY* that I believe that God had in mind from the beginning! Some of us have learned this the slow, hard way. I hope and pray that you will be a faster learned, for *life is so short! (And so fragile that it should be handled with. . . . . . . prayer!)*

What grandmother worth her salt would not talk of their grandchildren every chance she gets? Well, my dear Bill has two daughters, beautiful inside and out-and Christians-who have reared grand-children anyone would be proud of. And my two sons, Tim (a step-son) and Timothy (my birth child) are precious. Tim and Cathy have two boys. Perry and Drew, who are the cutest grandchildren you ever saw! (Does this sound like a prejudiced grandmother??? Well, *God has blessed me . . . and Bill, and . . . you?* (I hope!) Happy note: Sometimes inlaws and step-children can prove to be closer to you in ways that really count than many "blood" kin! There is unthinkable power in the human will, and there is un-dreamed-of goodness in *any* human heart that is cleansed by our Lord Jesus and who volunteers as a dwelling place for his Holy Spirit!

Some time ago, when I was a "single mom" a wreck happened right in front of me late one night on the freeway. I was O.K., but I got a debilitating migrane headache. I called Timothy and Cheryl. "We'll be right over" they said, asking no questions. They both spent the rest of the night helping me, with no regard for their loss of sleep and the next day's duties. They've been married 11 years and now expecting their first child! I can hardly wait! I have two exceptional sons who married lovely Christian girls who love our Lord. You see? *God is still blessing me!*

Bill and I have been married more than six years—the happiest years of my life. We visited many churches our first year together. Finally we attended where Bill had belonged before, out in Austell. After that first session in his old Sunday School class, the tremendous "at home" feeling I had, let me know why we had to wait and "shop around." I moved my membership there shortly, where we move among some of the finest Christian people I've ever known. *God is good!*

Breast cancer showed its ugly face in 1998. Bill and I have been through chemo and radiation together. And, I do mean *together!* You would have to know the tender, Christ-like compassion of my Bill to fully understand. He was right with me every step of the way. *God is still blessing me!*

When my Uncle Bob asked me to write this story, I knew I needed the help of our Lord, just as I have needed him all of my 60 years on his good earth. I want to live a long time yet and enjoy my precious family and friends. In that I'm just like the rest of you grandparents. But I have another "super" blessing I'd like to share with you. The first one is I Corinthians 2:9 "But as it is written, eye hath not seen, nor ear heared, neither have entered into the heart of man, the things which God hath prepared for them that love Him." Really now, our Lord Jesus has taken away my fear of death! And replaced it with *excitement* the *expectation* of an even better life with Him at his "home." Until then, another promise from Him is II Corinthians 12:9: "My grace is sufficient for you, for my strength is made perfect in weakness. "(K J V) Wow! Since we have this loving, gracious God who gave us his son, Jesus, and through Him everlasting life, what more could we ask or want? *And still God continues to bless me!* And all of us!

In His Great Love,
Judy Osborne 01/12/03

Editor's Postscript: Judy has faced one of America's biggest problems, and has given us some good, solid answers. Hear ye! The basic unit of *society* we call *"The Home"* has a crucial problem! To us who believe in marriage as a life-long commitment the great need is to *identify* and *fix* the *causes* of the breakdown. As perhaps you know, Christians are not exempt from any plague that afflicts society. But since we know the answers, then God, and society, should and will hold us responsible for *applying* and *sharing* those answers.

If you, or someone you know ever have to face the shock of divorce, for whatever reason, and your first reaction is "My life's dream is shattered. This is the end. I might as well just "give up.""

Don't fall for that "giv-up-itis" trick! Our fundamental, basic Christian belief in repentance, forgiveness, new life and a "new start" with the power of "Christ in you" (in the person of the Holy Spirit) is a sure defense against any perpetual loss or final defeat!

Assuredly, JRB

17

Peace at Eventide

—Carol J. Van Pelt

Rosemary, my special friend and neighbor—like so many—had an early encounter with cancer. It left her family and many friends with the agonizing expression, "Oh, no! not *her!*" Then would follow the several reasons why *she* should be exempted from the attack of the cruel killer.

She was too young to die. She was also a good, kind, and Christ-like woman. What would our community do without her? She was one of the *driving forces* for family fun in Albany. She loved attractive clothes and wore them like a queen. Rosemary was a beautiful woman, inside and out. She so enjoyed "Vintage clothes" that one Mother's Day she had a *fashion show* and had women and girls from the group as models. What fun we had!

We all thought Rosemary was taking the pounding of the disease—along with the usual periods of depression—quite well. After a round of chemotherapy, she and her husband, Dick, were able to take a special trip to visit family they hadn't seen in a long time. They were also able to celebrate their 50th Wedding Anniversary.

Eventually, however, her strength was spent and she returned to the hospital for the final stay. One of my last visits to see her in the hospital was especially memorable. I went in late morning, hoping few people would be around. Only Susie, her daughter, was there. I had met her on a previous visit and was glad for the chance to get better acquainted. At that earlier visit Rosemary was alert—laughing and having fun with "girl talk." She had asked about each of my family, one by one, and wanted to know how they were. [Rosemary always watched your eyes as you talked, which I considered a special gift. She would talk to you as if you were the only other person in the room.]

At this visit Rosemary was weak and pale. But she roused enough to exclaim over the roses and sweet peas I had brought from my garden. She said my name and thanked me sweetly. "Carol always knows just what I like," she whispered to Susie. I saw she was having trouble propping open her eyelids, so I assured her that she need not try to keep them open. Susie and I whispered back and forth as we held a hand on either side of the bed. We just sat quietly.

Then she began wrinkling her brow and moaning as if in pain. We pushed the button for a small dose of pain medicine. After being quiet for some time she began to rouse. We showed her the flowers again and she was so happy. She touched and smelled them, exclaiming over the colors, and repeated her earlier words, "Carol knows just what I like."

After another quiet period, she began talking. I had to lean close to understand her words. Not sure if she was talking to us or not, we just listened for a while. "You know" we heard her say, "I always wondered what it would be like when this time came, but it's not at all what I expected. Heaven isn't far off; *it's just a step away.* Oh, girls! It's so wonderful! I want you to come with me! So beautiful!"

Surprised at Rosemary's sudden forcefulness of voice and her insistence that we come along, I answered quickly: "O Rosemary, we *do* want to go too. Perhaps not today, but we *do* want to be there and see you again. Actually, it will be soon, and *we* will see what *you* are seeing!"

At this point she raised both her arms and said rather boldly, "Thank you, Father God, for these two precious people who are here to share this *special* day with me!"

It seemed to me that Rosemary was looking into the smiling face of God as she very personally gave thanks. After a moment Susie and I joined her in prayer, thanking God for this precious gift.

In my career as a nurse I have worked in about every phase of the job you can name, from nurse's aide to a "practitioner." I have seen many people pass out of this world. I have heard stories from relatives who have had family members speak of heaven as they were close to, "crossing over." But this was my first time of having such a "last visit on earth" like this with anyone. This time with my dear friend Rosemary was so *sacred* and *holy* that Susie and I could only whisper our *joy* and thank God for the privilege of being there.

—Carol J. Van Pelt

18

Angelic Surprise

—Martha L. Schaffer

Ours was a big, happy farm family where everyone did their share of the work in the house, garden and fields. Robbie and I were the two youngest. Our fertile farm was situated a few miles north of Bremen, Georgia.

By mid-summer hoeing the cotton and corn were finished. Our thoughtful Mother and Dad encouraged us to take our usual two-weeks "vacation** by visiting one of our married sisters in Atlanta, 50 miles east, before school started again. This summer it was our turn to visit Ruth. She always made plans for exciting things to do and educational places to visit in the big city. Among our favorite things were picnics, swimming, and good movies. Our joys were extended by telling our country cousins about our excursions when we returned home.

For me, this one summer was to be unforgettable for an unusual reason. Ruth's plan was to go to Grant's Park. First we would go swimming, then have a picnic on a grassy area, and climax the day by a visit to the park zoo. How exciting that sounded!

"Girls" Ruth said, "do you have your swim suits and everything ready to go?" We both responded affirmatively, and with eagerness. So she quickly finished packing that unique basket full of goodies and covered it with the red and while checkered oilcloth and away we went toward Grant's Park, not far from the Georgia State Capitol building. What I did not know was that my hopes of learning to swim would get a real "setback" that day.

As we went down the steps into the small section of the pool, Robbie headed for the tall sliding board, with me right behind her. Watching as she headed for the steps, I moved to the side to see her slide that ended in a big splash! Then she "dog-paddled" over to where Ruth was sitting on the cement partition of the pools. I planned to do the same thing. With enthusiasm I climbed the steps, sat down on the slide and zoomed down it, making a big *splash!*

As I started to dog-paddle over toward my sisters, I felt a strong current of water pull me to the left, then down and under the water. My sisters apparently did not notice my struggle in the water, hence they made no move to come and help me! I was excited, but the more I struggled the more the current seemed to pull me toward the bottom of the pool. It was hard to believe that I could so quickly be in such **real trouble**. I kept trying to get my head above water by pushing my toes against the bottom. Each time I came up a little it seemed that I was farther from my sisters. It seemed that a powerful force of water was sucking me away and I started to wonder where they would find my body when they missed me.

I fought for my life as long as I could, but after I sank to the bottom five times I knew I was drowning. Finally my strength was gone and I gave in to my fate. "I don't want to die" I thought. "But what else can I do?" I felt so *utterly alone!* I felt such pity for my family that I was about to leave.

Strangely enough, I did not panic! Suddenly there came a serene and soothing "*presence*" there in the water with me. Then from behind me there came an audible, low-pitched voice like that of a man, who gently asked: "Where are you going, little girl?" Assuming and hoping it was the voice of a lifeguard I thought, "Where do you think I'm going? I'm drowning!"

Then, to my *surprise* and great comfort, two strong hands from behind me gently reached under my arms and lifted me from the water. The next thing I knew I was sitting between my two sisters on the cement partition. I did not see my *"rescuer"* come nor did I see him go. Nor do I remember the trip across the water from where he found me to the place where my sisters were. It was as though I fell asleep in the water and awoke sitting between my sisters!

Sitting there I began shaking from head to toes, with my head pounding and bobbing from side to side. Robbie was sitting to my left and she turned toward me and excitedly asked, "Martha! What's the matter?"

All I could do was sputter out water and try to say through my gasps, "I almost drowned! And my head hurts!" That was all I even tried to say for a long time.

Soon my sisters jumped down into the water again, and Ruth presently announced that it was time for our picnic. Ruth still did not realize that I had almost drowned.

When we left the pool I noticed how difficult it was to lift one heavy foot after the other. But I remember nothing about the picnic lunch at all.

I do remember asking my sisters a few questions later, when I had gained enough strength to talk. "Ruth, did you see the man who rescued me from drowning?"

"No, Martha. What man?" was her response. At that point I did not realize that it was an *angel* that saved me. I had never heard of the possibility, hence it never entered my mind. The situation was too much for an eight-year-old to figure out. So for a long time I just figured that some man rescued me without my sisters seeing him, so they were not excited or concerned about it. I was almost afraid to tell them that I didn't see him either! But I knew that I had almost drowned and had been rescued! So I told my sisters: "I wanted so much to thank the man for what he did for me, but he left too soon."

Now that I am 75, and have lived what I consider, "The good life" of a Pastor's wife and helped my husband rear three wonderful and talented sons, (all college graduates) at my brother's *insistence* I have shared with you what I have wanted for years to share: God so loved the world that He not only gave us His Son, Jesus, to save us, (forgiveness of our sins and cleansing the very heart of us by His Holy Spirit) but He also gave us His book, the Bible, to instruct us! And as if it were some sort of a "bonus" God also gives us what we call, "Angels" to do for us what we cannot do for ourselves, just in the "nick *of* time" when we need help.

Long after the incident at Grant's Park in Atlanta, I no longer have to wonder why God does certain things, or why He is invisible, etc. But I rest in knowing God is good; He knows what He's doing. I have known many years that I really *do* have a, "guardian angel" (maybe for *emergency use only!*) That keeps me from presumption, or being cocky! I hope you like the few poems my dear brother, Robert Boggs, has in this book. I have news for you: He's as loving as his wife, Jodie, claims! In God's great *LOVE,—Martha L. Schaffer*

P.S. I was thankful in 1933. I'm still trying to catch up on thanksgiving to God, our gracious Father, for ALL His gifts of love.—MLS

19

Angels' Rescue Squad

—Laurie Dorgan

Jerry and I grew up in Illinois. Our families were Catholic. Jerry had thoughts of being a priest. I had thoughts of being a nun. I came from Berwyn, a town twenty minutes southwest of Chicago. Jerry grew up in one of the suburbs called Burbank. We met at work, and were married in January, right in the middle of the blizzard of 1979!!! We started a family with the birth of a son we named Josh, and a year later another son, Shawn, was born. We lived in Bolingbrook, Illinois at the time. In 1988 Jerry's job was ending there, and we were told he could have a job in Warsaw, Indiana. We came to visit and fell in love with the area. We soon moved.

There's quite a difference in living in the city and moving out into the country. We had a lot to learn. While Jerry was at work the children and I were busy learning how to get from "point A to point B." We made an adventure of it. We would get in the car and drive; get lost and then find our way back home.

On one of those excursions we went past a beautiful little country church. I remember making the comment that it was just the kind of church I was looking for. That summer a friend invited my boys to Vacation Bible School for children. It was *that* church; Pleasant Grove United Methodist! Our boys loved the VBS! The Pastor, Rev. Don Poyser, visited us, and made us feel welcome. For us it was a rapid succession of changes: A new area, new home, and a new church. Little did we realize how definitely our loving God was working in our lives.

Our daughter, Mackenzie, was born in November of 1989. She is the only born "Hoosier" in our family. In August of 1994 the Rev. Clyde Dupin came to Kosciusko County with a Billy Graham type county-wide Crusade. It was held in the High School Gym that summer. We had never attended one of those before, but attend we did, and our whole little family went forward to receive Christ as Savior and Lord. A retired minister, Rev. Robert Boggs, who attended Pleasant Grove, was assigned as our follow-up mentor. He came out to our house once a week for thirteen weeks of Bible study, and it was not too long until Jerry and I were lovingly calling him, "Dad Boggs" and soon the children were affectionately calling him, "Gran'pa Boggs."

God's Holy Spirit continued to work wonderfully in our family. A "Lay Witness Mission team" came to our church, and we felt drawn closer to our Lord, which continued to increase our spiritual appetite.

In 1997 our Mackenzie became very ill. She was hospitalized for a week with a mysterious virus. We almost lost her. At the same time Josh developed a serious ear infection. Both had to see the doctor at the same time. Josh also had to work that day. It turned out that Josh would have to drive to school to make it to the doctor's appointment and then to work. We were very nervous, but let him "fly." Josh made it to the doctor fine, and asked if we could pick up Shawn from school and bring *him* home before he had to go to work. I said "Yes."

Mackenzie and I were to get medicine for Josh and drop it off at his work. As we drove along I turned to a Christian Radio station by chance. We heard the song, "Our God is an Awesome God." We were excited because we had heard it first at the Lay Witness Mision! We rode along, singing it at the top of our voices.

God's Angels of Mercy

At that very same time. Josh and Shawn were in a terrible accident in our van. The van rolled over five times. The accident was on a gravel country road. Josh's glasses were ripped off his face and Shawn was badly hurt. Josh cannot see without his glasses, but heard his brother screaming and went running down the road looking for help. A couple came to help Josh and Shawn. They took Josh back to the van, found his glasses, helped Shawn and then as the ambulance appeared the couple *disappeared.* I'm convinced they were angels sent by God. The police assured us the boys were both very fortunate; that nobody should have survived such a crash. We know it was God who saved each of them. Looking back, we see that **we almost lost all three of our children in a two-week period of time.** But for God's great love and mercy, Jerry and I would have been left childless! No wonder that we, after these years, continue to listen to the station that "played our song" WBCL, Ft. Wayne, IN. It plays 24 hours a day, seven days a week!

God continues to work in great grace and mercy in our family. He has given us help and encouragement through lay workshops, our youth groups, concerts. Lay Academy, Bible Study and prayer, music, Christian Radio, and many *special people* He brings into our lives. I can't imagine how I ever got along living so far from Him, and can't imagine how empty life would be without Him! I love my Lord Jesus, and the wonderful husband He gave me, and the three precious children He gave *us* to love and rear for Him!

Life is a *continually unfolding adventure* of finding and doing God's will! I want to be a better wife and mother. As that happens, I will be a truly fulfilled and grateful person!—Laurie

20

Love Is Home-Grown

—Jodie Dean Boggs

Neither my husband Glen, nor I were Christians when we were married. After a few months I had a "change of heart." That meant I opened my life to Jesus Christ as my *Savior* and *Lord*. The change in me was a truly happy one, and I never got over it! I had such deep *joy* inside me that I could not keep silent about it. Before, I did not enjoy reading the Bible or going to church, but now both these things were a *thrill* to me. I was surprised that such a change was possible, in me *especially*.

For my young husband, Glen, the change in me was not a happy one. But to his credit, he did *tolerate* the "new" Jodie. That was about as far as he was willing to go. To my dismay he continued to put off a positive response to the claims of Christ on his life for 42 of the 43 years of our married life. For me the question lingered: "Why?" This led to a question many a spouse wrestles for years: "What is a 'believer' to do in that situation?"

I have never felt like saying, "Hey, follow me! I found the way and I have all the answers." Far from it. But if "it's the bottom line that counts" even if I stumbled, at least by God's grace I stumbled onto some answers in God's Word that worked for me. If you're interested, read on. The last year of his life on earth my Glen did come to a solid faith in Christ and a joyous assurance of eternal life. To me, that bottom line was the ultimate. Final triumph! Real joy at the finish line!

Two years after Glen died of cancer in 1998, I met the author, Robert Boggs, and was briefly relating my story to him. When I finished he said, "Beautiful! Not only is it a great story—you should put it on paper. There are *thousands* of people who have found themselves in a similar situation, and have wondered what to do. Your story could inspire and instruct others."

"I can't see how anyone could ever be inspired or learn anything from my simple little story. But if you're serious, I'll put it in writing." I did, and here it is!

Slowly I Learned and My Faith Grew!

It seemed to me that I was not a "fast learner" of what God's Book says about "submission" and "obedience." But maybe I made up for speed in *determination.* I knew that a wonderful change had come into my life. I also realized that I was a bit late with my own decision. But I was determined to hang onto this *new relationship* and make the best of what results this *new life* might bring.

I set no speed records, but grow in grace I did! I was faithful in Bible reading/church attendance, and *I never gave up! Going it alone* made for some low times, but I found the old proverb true: "One plus God is always a majority."

The old farm saying became meaningful to me: "You can lead a horse to water, but you can't make him drink." And this one on personal choice and responsibility: "God gave us each freedom to choose, and so far He has never revoked that freedom nor our responsibility for its use."

As I grew spiritually, I looked back and saw where I had failed to please our Lord by showing God's love and the respect due my husband. So desperate was I to see God change Glen that I failed to see how much *I* needed to allow God to keep making changes in *me!* Believing spouses, I think this is the proper place for changes to start! I know it is not what most of us want to hear, but . . .

This was what God finally got across to me. God wanted to change Glen, but the change needed first to start in me! Simple, but true. God had wanted to change Glen for so long that by the time the answer began, things seemed to be going downhill! It got so that Glen would hardly talk to me! I knew I must do something, but what? First I decided to stop going to church where I had been attending and spend two weeks just seeking God's will and direction for me.

With my Bible, a concordance, a dictionary, plus pen and paper, I studied the meaning of these words in the Bible: Obedience, honor, love, etc. Finally I found the key, and I promised God to share my discovery with Glen.

On a Sunday morning over our coffee I explained to my dear husband that God had shown me His plan for the head of the household to be the husband. I told him that I was now ready to stay in my God-given role while letting him do his part as the head.

To some extent I was already doing this, but my attitude I needed to change. As we quietly shared on that beautiful morning, the Holy Spirit let me see and feel the pressures I had long imposed on my mate. I saw a weight gradually roll off his shoulders. Then I saw a sweetness and tenderness come over him that I had never seen before! Yes, it was I who needed to change! And it began then and there!

I began doing things just to please Glen—without any fanfare or, hopefully, any hint of what I was up to. Of course the basic reason had to be to please and obey God, my Lord, in obedience to His Word. When I began to do everything "as unto the Lord" what I had hoped, dreamed, and prayed for began to come to pass. Surprise! It worked! As I did this (with the right motive and attitude) there came an increased flood of love, joy and peace into my own life that I had never imagined possible!

Why not try this: *don't 'ding-dong' your mate!*

Of all the little things you want him to do, don't say it twice. Request it clearly and lovingly—then drop it there! Time after time I tried this "say it only once" thing, and it worked! At times (after I thought he had forgotten) I just gave up my request/expectation/insistence. Then he would lovingly do what I had wished, and more! I compared this with the anger he used to display as a result of my hounding him about something I wanted. What a difference!

May I give a couple examples of "asking only once" and then giving it over to the Lord and prayer? We were remodeling our farm kitchen and living area. We had an island in the kitchen. Glen was ready to hang the light where he wanted it. I said: "I think I would like to have it directly over the sink at the island." About that time he excused himself to get some-thing from the barn. While he was gone I told the Lord that I really would like to have the light over the sink area in the island, but I refused to be fussy about it. "Help me . . . !"

When he returned from the barn he said "Jodie, I think I'll put that light over the sink area instead of the middle of the living area."

I was shocked at the speed and pleasantness with which our Lord had answered my prayer.

At another time Glen had me to call some friends and ask them to go with us out to eat at a fish place in Syracuse. Fish is not my favorite thing, but I did as he suggested. In my heart I said "Lord, it's been a long time since we've eaten at Peddler's Village in Goshen. I'd surely like to go there, but would you please speak to my husband about it?"

We picked up our friends and headed down their lane toward the road. Glen said: "I hope you all don't mind, but may I ask if it would be all right with all of you if we went to Peddlers' Village instead of the fish place?"

Wow! It reminds me of what some poet said a long time ago, "More things are wrought by prayer than this world dreams of." Really now, why fuss and fume about having your way about something when we can give it over to God and let Him decide it and do it His way? It's lots more fun!

And don't forget that if God's answer is "No" it's for a good reason, even if only to aid in our spiritual growth!

Ladies, by letting your husband have the "last word" in things, he carries the weight of responsibility for the outcome of the decision. If your husband is wrong, God will deal with him about it. By doing things God's way and showing the right attitude, your spiritual growth will be enhanced while your Christian joy will be more contagious!

Ladies, God does have the answers to life's questions if we just ask Him—and accept His answers! Yes, we can really love our spouse, even if he/she is not a Christian "believer." God really does answer our prayers—if we stay in deep, true love that is patient. (See I Corinthians, chapter 13.)

When my husband Glen died he was a true child of God! The last 11 months of his earthly life was the beginning of real life for him! God did such a beautiful work in his life during those 11 months that I, along with family and friends, could see that he was heaven-bound! It all started with God's great mercy and gracious love. But curiously, God waited years for me to understand—and practice—that real "home-grown love" that I needed to do as my part of the deal! Figure that one out, if you can. Fit it into your theology however you must, but I believe that is the reality we face.

After finding out that he had lung cancer, Glen wanted to attend Pleasant Grove church a couple miles north of our farm. The first Sunday we went, something personal and definite happened between Glen and the Lord. When we stood to sing, Glen let go of the hymnal. I turned and he was weeping. (I had never seen him cry before!) He held his hand over his heart. I asked if he had chest pains. He said, "No. I'm O.K." Later he asked if we might go to the altar to pray at the closing part of the service, and we did.

After lunch I could hardly wait to talk to him about what happened at church. I waited until he lay down to rest.

"Honey, may I ask what those tears at church meant?"

"Someone touched me" was his reply. Then he continued, "Now it's Jesus first, then others." What different talk from him! Before it was "Me first. If I don't look out for #1, no one else will." To hear him now say, "God first . . . ?"

The last eleven months of his final illness passed, and he witnessed about this wonderful "new life" to others. I could hardly believe what I was hearing!

During the last few weeks of his life one day he wanted me to lie down beside him. Putting out his arm for me to lie on he said, "Honey, you just don't know how much I love you!" What a precious moment!

Long time coming? Yes, but not too late! It was well worth the wait! I prayed—and asked for—this change in Glen almost 42 years earlier, and finally I saw it come to pass! He witnessed to our daughters Gerry, and Ronda, and to our son, Michael, about the love, peace, and joy he received in his heart that Sunday morning at Pleasant Grove United Methodist Church.

The Holy Spirit of God touched him, lifted him up in His loving arms and flooded him with His peace, joy and love. Glen assured all who would listen that God would do the same for them if they would just do what he did—surrender their lives to Jesus the Savior! When Glen left us in December of 1998, the deep assurance of knowing where and with Whom he went overshadowed the "valley of the shadow of death" with a glory!

What a joy it was for me, that after 43 years, persevering love finally won and Glen could also enjoy the great "prize" of eternal life with Jesus! The answer is worth the wait!

My word to you men and women with an unbelieving spouse is "hang in there" with love that is faithful and genuine. God is faithful, and so must we be. Yes, God must be first. That is the only right place to start. Make it your aim to lay aside your petty notions and look at God's promises to all who put Him first. Why not buy one of those little books with God's promises listed by category? God's "special people" are those who take Him and His word seriously. Remember: Love is home made. Love is so central that the Bible says, ". . . God is love . . ." as we read in I John 4:16. You can "take that to the bank" along with St. John 3:16 in any version you choose! "And let us not be weary in well doing, for in due season we shall reap if we faint not." Galatians 6:9 (KJV,

Holy Bible.) Want some more "pure joy"? Get your Bible and read Romans 5:3–4; 8:25 and 10:8–13.

May I share with you what I consider a "bonus" for the measure of faithfulness on my part? After my husband had been gone two years I was lonely. I talked it over with our Lord. I asked Him if He would please give me another husband. One who would, first, love God with all his heart; second, love me for me; third, one who likes to travel, and fourth, one who enjoys good, healthful food as I do.

Guess what? About two years ago God had me meet the Christian writer, Robert Boggs. He met all four of those qualifications, and more!

Faithfully he loved and cared for his first wife, Maxine in her 16-year battle with Alzheimer's. She went home to be with her Lord on May 22, 2000. Their marriage was sweet and beautiful, even during the agonizing last few years of her illness. Robert's first book, *I'll Move Over, The Story of a Great Love,* describes something of the agony and the *glory* of those years.

Robert and I were happily married on March 31, 2,001, and enjoyed a beautiful 5-week honeymoon. We've decided to declare, by faith, the rest of our life together "an extended honeymoon." We often have what we call, "little dates." The whole month of August, 2002, we've had a glorious trip from Indiana to California, Oregon, and back again, seeing family, friends, and parts of God's vast creation that reflect His majesty—so awesome we were often silenced with the breathless wonder of it all. Neither of us can remember worshipping our great Creator-Sustainer God so much, so often!

So-o-o, you want to know how it is to live with this man—this honest, true, "born-again" Christian? In one short word "Fantastic!" If you want one more word it would be "Marvelous." I marvel at this guy every day! I'm beginning to see the exalted idea God had in mind when He planned marriage. I see a big difference in what we are experiencing and what many other marriages around us look like.

I'm trying to tell you what I have experienced the past 19 months—and not embarrass my husband or have you think I "dreamed it up!" I'm having a struggle to describe it! My Robert really is a "dream come true." We women want to be loved and respected. Picture, if you can, a husband who often tells you he loves you—most any time, seven days a week!

You've heard: "Love is blind?" It must be, because when Robert tells me I'm beautiful I tell him he's blind. I can't say he's lying, because I believe he's a truthful man.

O well, I still can't get used to it—after 19 months! Picture this, if you can: an exchange of hugs and kisses throughout the day, seven days a week! It makes our marriage well, *real* fun!

Robert opens the car door for me—or any door! He takes no credit for it. He says any credit goes to his old Irish Dad for teaching him women are, "special." Says that's how he was brought up. That's how he was taught to treat his mother and ten sisters, therefore he just doesn't know any better! (You want to know a little secret? He has me looking for him when he happens not to be with me! Then I realize he's not with me and I have to do it myself. Isn't that sweet?)

Contrast that with a woman who had back trouble for three days and had to crawl to the bathroom because her husband was angry at the situation she was in. My husband wants to stay pretty close to me just in case I need him. (Like a recent bout with leg cramps.)

Some of you are waiting for "the other shoe to drop" as I say that every marriage has "adjustments" whether it's a first or second. You're right! I had to adjust to his tendency to drive a little faster than I tend to. And he looks at the gas gauge differently. If it gets below 1/2 tank, I begin looking for a gas station. Not Robert. He seems more interested in the price at the pump than how near empty it is. No, we don't often run out of fuel, but pretty close at times, which has led to some very interesting situations!

And it's amazing how small a kitchen is to me when two people are in it! I never had the problem before, and it takes some getting used to. I love it though. It means that Robert is preparing one of his interesting "concoctions" that I do not have to think up. Some of 'em aren't bad! It's just that one has to cultivate a "taste" for new things. I had a big kitchen at the farm for years, and still knew where everything was. Glen had no interest in the kitchen or housework. Now it's like *our* kitchen! We're having fun adjusting, and making progress, really, and both know it was God who brought us together.

I asked God for a Christian husband—one who loved to travel. I have probably traveled more in these 19 months than in all the rest of my 69 years put together. We've gone from Lake Superior to Miami (and the Bahamas) and from Washington D.C. to southern California. Then up the coast to Oregon and back, visiting family and friends, *and* what must surely be many of the most awesomely beautiful parts of this good earth our great God has created! We spent the whole of August loving family and friends. And worshipping our great Creating/Redeeming/Saving God!

Maybe your husband only hugs/kisses you once a week or when he *wants* something. If he's like that, you probably can count on one hand the little helpful things he does around the house in a whole week. At your house does each try to, "out-do each other" in loving deeds? Do you practice *forgiving* little short-comings "until 70 × 7"? (Too often to count!) We do—we have to! And it all contributes to the genuine fun we're having! Neither of us can imagine what God has in store for us in the years ahead, but judging from the first 19 months, it has to be beautiful! Robert's a great lover, a wonderful father, grandfather, & great-grandfather. And I'm married to him! All praise and thanks to our Lord!!! (And God loves us all the same—showing no partiality!)

Let me close by saying: Robert and I wish for all of you the same fun, beauty and joy we're having in our home—and that's fantastic!

I must not forget to tell you that I have hurt Robert a few times. Not so much by my words but by how I answer him, i.e., the tone of my voice. This is where I need to be more like Christ our Lord. That's the part of me God and I are still working on! And I'm so glad God "isn't finished with me yet!" Rest assured that through it all Robert keeps on loving me still, just like Jesus does! I'm praying for each of you who read these words, and I ask you to pray for me.

I wish each of you could really come to know my Robert—and our Lord Jesus! You would love them both!

21

The Perfect Flight Until...!

—Dr. Doug Carter

Edited by J. Robert Boggs

02/23/02 Lakeland, FL. We heard Dr. Doug Carter speak again today at the camp meeting on S. Florida Avenue here in Lakeland. Delightful time! If I live to be 100 I think I will still remember the story he told so expertly. He reminded us that Jesus Christ was the *Master Storyteller* of all history, and that he told stories, or parables, for more than one reason.

Number one, he wanted people to remember what he said and taught. I met Dr. Carter later in the Dining Hall and asked him for permission to share his story in this book. He graciously gave his permission. The incident happened when he was President of Circleville Bible College, south of Columbus, Ohio.

Years earlier, he and his wife, Winnie, served as missionaries to a great people, our own American Indians, out in Arizona. Lately he has served as Pastor-at-large for World Gospel Mission out of Marion, Indiana, with "the world as his parish" as he (and John Wesley) put it. I would like some day to edit and publish a whole book of his stories. Better yet, maybe he will!

Now let me switch to first person as we sit at the feet of a truly great story-teller who specializes in *true stories from real life*, Dr. Doug Carter. First he

read a Bible story you can find in St. John 21:15–19.
Then he led into this powerful personal story:

It was a beautiful spring day—April 14, 1988. I had
been the speaker at a series of meetings at the United
Methodist Church in Spartanburg, South Carolina.
Now I was eager to get back to my desk at the Bible
College in Ohio. I took one of those little "connector"
flights from Spartanburg to Charlotte, N.C. The schedule was tight and I was rushing through the terminal
when I had an almost uncontrollable urge to stop at
the gift ship for a card for my precious wife, Winnie,
and souvenirs for the three children. Fortunately the
first card I picked up was *perfect* for Winnie. Nearby
was a rack of refrigerator magnets with names. The
top one said: "Angie is a Superkid" which I grabbed for
our Angie. Top of the next row said the same thing for
Eric! I took that one. Third row, top, had the same message for Jason! (I wondered how many hundred years
it might be until I could shop for my four "special people" in less than five minutes again!) Then I dashed on
to my waiting jet to board for Columbus. Whee! I buck-
led my seat belt and probably whispered, "Thank You,
Lord Jesus!"

As I reached for the book I planned to read on the
way, I relaxed as the Captain came on and greeted us,
saying it looked like a *perfect day* for a *smooth flight*
and we should be safely on the ground in Columbus,
Ohio in about 41 minutes! I rejoiced again for safe
flights in perfect weather.

Soon we climbed to 35,000 feet into the blue sky
with a lovely carpet of green under us. Presently the
Captain came on again, with his special Tarheel English, and told us we had just crossed the border into
West Virginia and how many minutes it would be

until we touched down at Columbus. I settled into my book again. . .

The *suddenly* there was a loud EXPLOSION! It reminded me of the dynamite blasts my Dad used to do in blowing up tree stumps at the farm in south Georgia. It was *deafening!*

The plane began to lurch and tremble, with a rush of air through the cabin that was absolutely *terrifying!* I looked behind us. Where the Rest Room had been was now a BIG HOLE in the side of the plane. I looked out the window and one of the engines was missing. It had exploded and blown a hole in the plane, taking out the rest room and making a small hole in the other side of the plane. The oxygen masks dropped down, but there were not enough of 'em, so some people started fighting for them. The pain in our ears over the sudden loss of air pressure was indescribable.

Sound effects? How can I describe the yelling, screaming, cursing and praying I heard in those few moments. The man right behind me was the loudest. He must have been an atheist, because he cursed God and called him some of the most vulgar names you can imagine and lots I had never heard. Then he would take off his mask and pray to that same God as loud as he could. Next thing he would be cursing again. I remembered what Jesus said about what's inside us *will* come out! It will, in a crisis or unguarded moment.

The food carts came reeling down the aisle and pinned two of the flight attendants against a wall, cutting a big gash in the head of one fellow. One girl looked almost as white as a sheet. (We learned later that this was the first flight for some of these young people after their training and orientation!) Piedmont Airline, flight #486! What a beginning!

The next few seconds seemed like a *l i f e t i m e.* Muffled voices from all directions, some cursing but most were crying out to God for mercy, as we headed down toward what *was* a beautiful carpet of green. *Now* the same trees were getting closer and the mountain forests looked like the *jaws of death* that would soon open to consume us! From listening to those prayers, I had a strange feeling it might be the first time some of them had ever prayed. It's a helpless feeling to be headed with breakneck speed toward what looks like your sure death. "This is it" I thought. Strange thought: "I wonder where I'll be buried?" I really don't want to leave my Winnie and children. My work for God I didn't think was finished. Being burned to a cinder in a fiery crash wasn't the ending I had hoped for. If there's not enough left of my body to identify, I guess they'll just have a "memorial service." Where will it be held? And who will lead it? What will they say at the service?"

Strange thoughts in what may be one's last moments? Not at all. If you had been in that plane, you would think them too. My reason told me that, without some very unusual miracle, we were *all* facing *certain* death, and that in just a matter or seconds, or minutes at the most.

Amid all the confusion and noise of the crisis, I cannot tell you what was in the minds and hearts of the others on that craft, but let me, as humbly and honestly as I know how, share with you some things, deep inside me, I experienced in those moments. Knowing that each of you will, in some way, face what is your big crisis, I beg you to listen carefully:

I looked around me with pity I cannot describe. I was *so* sorry they had made wrong choices that made their final moments so terrifying. For them I had pity and a helpless feeling. But when I looked into my own heart I found overwhelming *thankfulness* that I had chosen to trust and follow Jesus as my Savior and Lord. In contrast to the guilt, bitterness and *raw fear* I saw around me, I looked deep in my heart and there was *indescribable peace! Love!! And Joy!!* All this, when, with one glance out the window I saw what looked like certain death for me and all others on the plane.

I thought, "The old-timers were right! This peace the world didn't give me and nothing on earth can take it away—not even death."

It seemed like a miracle to me. I had actually come to the "finish line" with no apologies to make, no unsettled scores I wished I had settled! There was *no unfinished business* with my wife, family, friends, or God that I need to attend to! Mind you, I didn't *want* to die. I wanted very much to live. But I was completely at rest in the presence of the God I had served all those many years of my life! Mind you, I'm not bragging. I'm just telling you what was taking place in my most grateful heart during the closing seconds and minutes of what I thought would be the last line on my last page!

I experienced in those fast-paced moments the wonderful, incredible, loving, and *overflowing peace* that comes from the loving heart of God! *God was with me!* The same faithful God I had served for many years!

While this incredible peace and joy flooded my soul, I looked down at my briefcase and thought of the card for my Winnie and the refrigerator magnets I had found for Angie, Eric and Jason when I was in such a hurry to catch this plane. Suddenly I added my prayer to all those I was hearing in muffled tones around me. In my heart I said: "Lord, I'm not asking you to save my life at this point. But it would be great if You would protect my briefcase so Winnie could read that sweet card and she and the children could know they had first place in my heart on the last day of my earthly life. Lord, You protected those three Hebrews in the fiery Babylonian furnace, and you can protect that briefcase today so someone can find it and take it to my Sweetheart wife, Winnie. That's all I ask."

Now, friends, may I tell you what the Holy Spirit then said to me, ever so gently and yet very forcefully: *"Doug, if Winnie and the children do not already know they have high priority in your life, one card and three refrigerator magnets is too little, too late."*

Wow! So truthful, so gentle, and yet so forceful a message in a crisis moment! Dear ones, it tells me that our children and our grandchildren need some of our *time* more than anything. More than gadgets, money, or any earthly thing, our family and friends need a little of *us* and *our time.* Why not now lovingly focus some quality time and invest it in the people you really care about? Don't wait until the crisis! Don't come up with "too little too late." Do it now! Now! The inheritance of real value you leave is not money/things. The true values you can give is holy living, Godliness, a life of loving and prayerful investment of time, given while there's still time!

When we passengers thought our end was a matter of a few seconds, the voice of our Captain finally came on. "Folks, our plane is badly damaged. But, if I can get over this next mountain ridge, I want to try landing it on the airfield in the next valley. I will do my best. All I ask of you is prayer."

We *did* miss the ridge, and he settled the jet down on the runway and came to a screeching halt at Charleston, W. Va. (Said to be the most severely damaged plane to ever land safely.) Suddenly we were surrounded by men in strange-looking suits.

They checked us thoroughly for explosives. The man behind me jumped into the aisle and yelled: "It's Miller time!" But the couple next to me said, "We'll be in church next Sunday!" They later said they had not been in church since their daughter was married 25 years ago. We finally were moved into the Terminal where one corridor was turned into an emergency room with doctors, nurses, and yes, the news media. In the hours that followed I was privileged to counsel almost every passenger on the plane, I think. I had the joy of praying with the couple who said they would be in church the next Sunday, and they both confessed their faith in Jesus Christ as their Savior and Lord, along with quite a number of others. So far as I learned, I was the only Christian in the plane at the start!

About a third of us elected to take another flight they offered, while the rest chose other ways home.

Finally I was back home, greeted my Winnie more passionately than ever, I suspect, and was at my desk sorting the pile of mail. In the door walked our Chief of Maintenance. (Years ago he was the town drunk. Some college students led him to Jesus, and he became a real staunch Christian). He was weeping. "What's the matter Willie?" I asked.

"Well Chief, I'm not sure. Were you in some sort of trouble earlier today?"

"Well, you might call it that. I had a very unusual experience this morning. I hope I never have another like it. Why?"

"Well, this morning I was over in the academic building with a florescent bulb over my shoulder to install in one of the classrooms before class. As I stepped into the room the Holy Spirit spoke to me about an urgent need to pray for you." 'O.K. I said. I'll change this light bulb and go right back and pray.' "

The inner voice said, "Willie, that will take too long—it will be too late. You need to pray now. It's absolutely urgent to pray at this moment."

So I looked over at the Professor and said, "I feel an urgent burden to pray for the President of our college. I believe he's in trouble. I don't know where he is or what he's doing, but I just know God wants us to pray for him. Would it be O.K. with you if we prayed?"

The Prof. said, "Let's pray." To the students he said, "Would you like to join us in prayer right now?"

So we all got down on our faces and began to pray. He said later: "I couldn't think of any words to pray except these: *'O God, the President is in trouble. Would you stretch forth Your mighty arm and hold him in the palm of Your hand, and protect him in his hour of need!'*"

By then I was weeping. He had no idea I was at 35,000 feet at that hour over West Va. when they were praying at Circleville, Ohio! I filled Willie in, and finally got back to my mail, paying special attention to the "one book" (my desk calendar), God's Holy Spirit had suggested I look into.

That evening I'm at home, sitting in my living room, reviewing the day and thinking of all that had happened. I said, "Lord, You could have protected us, and You could have delivered me, if Your servant Willie had failed to pray, but. . .And suddenly I felt a check in my spirit, as if I had said something incorrect. So I thought about it for a while, and then the message came through clearly to me—you can draw whatever conclusion you wish—but the Holy Spirit said to me: "Doug, the God of Heaven does some things in answer to prayer that He will not do for any other reason."

I believe that I'm alive today because *that man*, (and I later learned some others) were burdened to pray for me at *that very hour*, 10:00 a.m.

Some time later I got a letter from an 88-year old woman in Southern Alabama. She was out in her yard working with flowers when a burden of prayer come over her. She said, "Yes, Lord. I'll go pray as soon as I get these flowers finished." But the "inner voice" said, "Now." So she laid down her tools, went in beside her bed and prayed for me.

Later she wrote, with shaky handwriting, "Doug, I'm getting old and my memory fails me at times. I'm occasionally mistaken about things, but I just wanted you to know that about 10 a.m. on April 14, I was praying for you. I prayed: "God, reach forth your Mighty arm, hold him in your Mighty hand and protect him in his hour of need." [Did you notice the same words of the Maintenance Man in Ohio at the same hour prayed about 750 miles apart?] "That's awesome" as I've heard some young people say these days.

My aged friend had no idea I was flying at all. I have shared this with you to make this point: Life will have its "suddenly's" for us all, but if we give our lives to God, walk with Him, and steadfastly purpose to do His will (trusting Him moment-by-moment), even when the "BIG ONE" comes, whatever it is, Jesus can give you a deep peace inside. With Him you can overcome *anything* in the power of His might!

Don't forget to order your priorities wisely, and avoid regrets later. Remember, you are now determining what will be said at your funeral by the way you live every day. Finally, God *does* answer prayer. He actually does move in miraculous ways in answer to the prayers of His trusting, obedient children! Not everyday will God ask you to pray for someone in an aircraft about to explode. But maybe you need to pray for someone you've about given up on. Restoring broken lives is very important to God. One common ingredient in every miracle: Each starts with a need—problem—a crisis—someone in trouble—someone who needs God's loving intervention!

22

Insights on Islam

—Dr. Thomas Hermiz

Let me share with you something that lies close to my heart. One that ought to lie close to yours. It is the tremendous, enormous unfinished task we Christians have of reaching the people of Islam—those who profess to be followers of Allah. If there is any group of people in the world that the Church has failed to impact and to reach, it is the Muslim people. We are paying the price, and will continue to pay a high price for our neglect.

What I'm sharing with you is not something that has been on my heart just since 9/11. Those who have heard me speak at missions gatherings over the years know that I have tried to challenge people with the pressing need of taking the Good News of Jesus Christ to the Muslim people. For 12 years I have tried to communicate the burden that God would give us someone in World Gospel Mission, and in the Churches of Christ in Christian Union, who would feel a very specific, definite *call* to take the Gospel to Muslim people.

It was not until Paul and Kerri Jenkins came along a few years ago and committed themselves to this ministry that we had the first real *breakthrough*. My prayer is that this will be just the beginning of a great increase of a real concern and burden for the Muslim people of the world.

Before proceeding further, I want to pause and refer you to a "back to the basics" Scripture for my being a "concerned Christian" in our shaky, uncertain world. The reference is St. John's Gospel, 14:6. It is one of those places we find a clear record that tell exactly who Jesus was and why he came to "planet earth." I will quote the verse for you later on. Let me tell you now about my "family credentials."

My father was born and raised until the age of 10 in the country of Turkey. His parents had immigrated there from Iraq. They were Asyrians. When he was five years of age Muslims from that part of the world were on one of their many "Jihads" and were determined to wipe out Christians from that region.

Many in our family were Christians. My grandmother, my great grandparents, and my aunts and uncles had been led to the Lord by American missionaries from the state of Kansas, U.S.A.

My grandfather formed a little army and was going around trying to defend these Christian villages against the Muslims. Finally they "put a price" on his head and he had to escape the country. He finally landed in America, planning, as soon as he was settled, to send for his family. But very shortly he received the message that his entire family had been massacred by the Muslims. That message was *almost* true.

I say "almost" true, because the day they invaded the village of of Midyak where my father, five years of age, lived with his mother, his grandparents and his sister—twenty-eight members of his family died that day as martyrs for their faith in the Lord Jesus Christ—slain by Muslim people.

But a Muslim soldier took the little boy, who later became my father, off the street to his home. From the time he was five until he was ten years old he lived in so many different Muslim and Christian homes he cannot remember all the different places he lived. Finally an uncle found him and kidnapped him, then got him out of the country and sent him to America! All this I tell you so that you will know my family have close and firsthand knowledge of what Islamic fundamentalists are like. I have also had a unique opportunity to observe them in many parts of the world for the last 25 years.

I have a concern now that what we are being told about Muslims leaves a gap between what we hear and the facts we need to know and face. Much of it seems to be just an effort to be, "politically correct." News media where we're supposed to get "facts" is, again, the big offender. And even our own President at times says things that are politically "correct" but not factual.

Please understand: Islam is both a religion and a political system. And, they have the objective of *controlling the world*. At this moment they control the lives of 1 1/2 *billion* people. And they are growing by 50 million people a year. It is now the fastest-growing religion in the world.

It is a religion based on "works." It gives no real hope/assurance of *eternal life*. Except, perhaps, a couple things that "might" help you in the next life. One, you hope that your good deeds outweigh your bad one. And one big point: Be sure the very last thing you do in this life is a *good work*. According to Muslims, the very best of "good works" is to kill an infidel. No, I'm not kidding! And if you, in Jihad, or "holy war" kill an infidel, it just about guarantees you "eternal life." They are taught this from childhood.

So *that* is why young men and women are willing to strap bombs on their bodies and go into places where Jews or Christians congregate and kill as many of them as possible, along with themselves. As ridiculous as that seems to us, they really believe that. (When you hear people say it doesn't matter what you believe as long as you're sincere, don't listen!) Some of these young men are being offered not only assurance of Paradise, but as many as 70 virgins there to attend to their every need!

Down through the centuries Christian people have been dying for their faith in Jesus Christ. When these young Muslims die, they take a non-Muslim with them into death, with glowing promises of "favors" in life after death. Their passion is to bring all the world under Islam, and their government. There is never any religious tolerance or freedom.

When they are in control it is *against the law* to practice any other faith or religion. If you are caught trying to convert a Muslim to another faith, and are convicted, the penalty is death, or a long prison term.

Our news media, for some reason, would have us believe Muslims believe in peace. But their concept of peace is when a whole city, nation or the whole world is under their control! That's a long way from ours! All you have to do is read history, or your newspaper or watch TV news! Theirs is a very oppressive society that will not tolerate Jews or Christians. If they are peace-loving, why don't they release from their hot, rat and vermin-infested prisons all over the world the thousands of Christians and Jews they detain this very day?

Yes, not all Muslims would approve what took place on September 11. But there are more than 150 million Muslim Fundamentalists in our world. They seek absolute control via oppression and force. As I speak to you today, they are murdering thousands of Christians every day. Where? In the Sudan, in Saudi Arabia, in Indonesia, and in Pakistan. And they fully expect that, one day, they will rule the world! Why do they hate us? Because we're not Muslims. And because we support Israel. They are using terrorist attacks to try to frighten us away from supporting Israel. Fear and hate are their two big weapons. Americans may be harder to scare than other nations. We shall see. Isn't that a poor way to make converts? Another question: Why do those who teach their children and youth to die for their "Allah" run and hide in caves like frightened rats following their cowardly acts?

Let me remind you: There's still a covenant with Israel God made a long time ago: "I will bless those who bless you and curse those who curse you." It's very interesting to me that when the former President Clinton would have discussions with the PLO or Arafat and pressure Israel to make decisions not in their best interest, every time there were bad "natural disasters" is in Arkansas! And now, I have noticed that when Pres. George W. Bush puts pressure on Israel to move away from their historic positions, Texas has had some very bad "natural" disasters. Maybe it "just happened" but it is interesting. We all know what happened on 9/11, but do you know that on 9/12 Secretary of State Colin Powell had been scheduled to present to the United Nations a proposal to 1) Recognize a Palestinian State and 2) To move Israel's borders back to what they were prior to 1967 War? I don't need to tell you there would be no way Israel could defend themselves with those borders! We must not let Muslim blackmail back us away from supporting Israel. I'm not saying that everything Israel does is right, proper and correct. But we simply need to be reminded of what this whole thing it about. Did you know there are now three times as many Muslims in the United States as members of the Assemblies of

God? More Muslims in the United Kingdom than all the Methodists and Baptists combined! There are 7 million practicing Muslims in the United States. Some Black leaders said: "Islam is the religion of Black people. Christianity is a White man's religion." Many believed the big lie!

All this started in 610 A.D. by the man Mohammed. He said he had "revelations from God" via Gabriel, the Archangel. After these "visions" he would fall on the ground and foam at the mouth. This tells us he was a demon-possessed man, which may explain why so much hatred and evil in that religion. Mohammed had 12 wives and several concubines. One of these wives was 12 years old. If he had lived in America he would have been in jail, where he should have been early on. He got someone to write down the "messages" in Arabic after he would have one of his "spells." Later they were collected and put into what they call the "Koran." The Muslim clerics tell us that you can't really understand the Koran unless you can read Arabic. Not many people read Arabic, so maybe that's the reason their clerics control so big a multitude of people! Talk about "blind faith"!

Many of us have read both books and also compared the god they call "Allah" and Jehovah, or YHWA or some such Hebrew abbreviation. No matter what those who want to be *"Big Hearted"* or "politically correct" may say, "any way you shake it" the Allah of the Koran is *not* the God we find in our "Holy Bible!" Aside from names, their God is a ***very angry*** God: Unknowable, unapproachable, and untouchable. There is no provision for forgiveness of sins, hence, no conviction for sin. You can do just about anything you want to do, so long as your "good deeds" outweigh your, "bad deeds." If you're a man who travels and you want to take a "temporary wife" you are free to do so.

Muslims want to take over big cities. London is their first goal. They believe if they take London, the rest of Europe will be easy. Some of you have wondered why America cannot get the support we need in our time of need. Europe is so filled with Muslims they *cannot* support us—openly, at least. It is not only that Europe is dependent on Arab oil but when it comes to a body-count they are already at the "hard place" we are fast approaching! We have practically ignored our borders and immigration law so long that it may almost be too late to begin to enforce *anything* any more.

Since 622 A.D. Muslims have raped, murdered, and slaughtered every Christian and every Jew they could get their hands on! Now, every 15 days Muslims are killing 7,000 Christians somewhere in this world. In Sudan alone, over the last two years they have massacred more than two million Christians. I'm disturbed!

I'm disturbed that, after 9/11 when we can have a 3-hour "prayer service" in Yankee Stadium and the name of Jesus is not mentioned from the platform even once, in one prayer! (And Christians are suppose to be an 86% majority in this country?)

I'm disturbed by all the people in the entertainment world and the news media to *hate* Jerry Falwell and hate Pat Robertson! No, millions of us Americans don't always like all they do and say, but many seem to hate them more that they hate Saddam Housein or Suma Bin Laden! Hate shows!

The Bottom line, having spoken a lot of "rugged truth," what should be our attitude toward Muslim people?

Answer: It should be the same as toward every person, *we must love them*. That means we will treat them *right*.

It disturbs me when I see anyone or any group *burning their mosques!* Or painting swastikas on Jewish Synagogues, or any other personal or group action that is not in keeping with the *Golden Rule* our Lord Jesus laid down for us:

> **"So in everything, do to other what you would have them do to you, for this sums up the Law and the Prophets."**
>   (St. Matthew 7:12 NIV, Zondervan)

So, settle it in your heart that you will treat everyone with courtesy, kindness, and the kind of love Jesus has shown to you! Whoever your neighbors, treat them according to the "Golden Rule" Jesus gave us! Jesus is color-blind. He also refuses to notice class and economic distinctions. He ministered to the down-and-out *and* and up-and-out. He did not cowtow to the rich nor did he avoid them. He did not look down on the poor. He bent down to help them, like He did everyone else who needed Him.

But please do not bring heretical sect leaders onto your church platform! Try to avoid any act that would legitimize what you know is wrong. This might seem like a straight and fine line for leaders at times, but I believe it is important. Our Lord Jesus said: *"I am the Way, the Truth, and the Life. No one comes to the Father except through me"* St. John 14:6 (NIV, Zondervan). Heretical cults are *not* our "brothers/sisters!

Be ready, Christians, to walk in the doors of opportunity God gives us! Some of you remember when Japan surrendered to us? The whole nation suddenly knew that their Emperor was *not* God, after all, and they asked for 1,000 Christian Missionaries! General Douglas McArthur passed the call on to all the churches of America. We only mustered a few dozen! How embarrassing! Now we are praying for our great, loving God to put down hate, evil and falsehood and exhalt truth and righteousness. Do we believe He can and will?

What if the Arab world were to suddenly discover their "Allah" is colossal fraud and his devotees want to become followers of our Lord Jesus by the millions? How ready would we be for such a "harvest"? We made one colossal mistake last century, and many of us remember it. Now less than 1% of the people of Japan are Christians! What an opportunity we let slip. Let's pray and then get ready for God's answer! Believe the word of our omnipotent God!

I remember praying a few months ago with a little Muslim girl at a school where I was teaching. She had been there only a little while thus exposed to Christianity a short time. She came forward to the Altar to ask Jesus to come in and take all her heart. I remember what she said to me: "I've been here only a little while, and I've fallen in love with Jesus. I love him so much!"

Then she said, "Do I have to give up my Muslim religion?"

I could tell her with confidence that our Christ Jesus was so much greater and so much more wonderful there would be no room in her heart for any other religion! Assuming that you have found Jesus to be as wonderful as I have, all we need to do is pray for people and ask God to convict them of their need and emptiness without Him. When they know our forgiving, loving Lord Jesus, he will become everything to them, just as he has for all who get to really know Him!

Christians in America spend 1/10th of 1% of our church income on getting the Gospel out to the Muslim world! 96% of what *we* give is spent right here at home on ourselves and our programs!

Let me tell you the story of my Dad's last trip back to the middle-east he had left when he was a 10-year-old boy. At 83, he and mother took one last trip back to Midyad, Turkey. On that trip they opened a church there in his old home town that his grandfather had built. It had been closed for years, and they were ready to turn it into a factory!

My Dad went to the authorities and told them they couldn't do that! It was built by his father and was dedicated to the preaching of the Gospel. They said didn't know that, and they said, "It's yours." So he and my mother went in and dusted off the pews, and then went up and down the streets and invited the people. (Some of whom had been involved in the massacre of his family 73 years before!) And they came!

As he was leaving Istanbul he met a cousin that he did not know he had and learned he was a born-again, spirit-filled minister of the gospel! He said he did not know there was a church in Midyad, and promised Dad and Mom he would see to it, some how, some way, that the church stays open! What an incredible trip they had!

On the flight home, sitting right next to Dad was a Muslim. For six hours he had a "captive audience." He gave his testimony, and shared Christ with the man. They were about an hour out of Philadelphia and my father, who in his later years became probably the greatest one-on-one soulwinner I have even known, said to himself: "I have been sharing Jesus with this man about five hours now, and I think it's about time I invited him to pray and as Jesus into his heart."

Dad turned toward the man to ask, but before he could speak the man said, "You have been sharing with me about this Jesus for five hours. I wondered if you would pray with me now. I want to ask this

Jesus Christ into my very heart. I want him in my life to. Would you?"

For that last hour my dear Dad, in his heart was flying about ten thousand miles high in joy for the privilege of leading a hungry-hearted Muslim to the feet of Jesus.

Friends, people are hungry for Jesus! His perfect love drives out fear, and a lot of other "stuff" we don't need and don't want inside us! Jesus in the, "Perfect Everything" each one of us *need*, including Muslims. If you don't have Him, ask Him to come into the very center of you. If you already have Him, try sharing Him with others!

Sincerely,
Thomas Hermiz

23

Tough Circumstances?
Never Give Up!

A Review of "A Charge To Keep"
by George W. Bush
by the editor J. Robert Boggs

The title for this last chapter came from my re-reading George W. Bush's book, *A CHARGE TO KEEP* which he copyrighted in 1999 and published by the William Morrow and Company, Inc., 1350 Avenue of the Americas, New York, N. Y. 10019.

I asked permission to use extensive quotes from the book because I want you, my fellow Americans, to know the *real* George W. Bush, as I feel that I know him by a thoughtful re-reading of his book.

I want to start in Austin, Texas, in the back yard of the Governor's Mansion. Please stay with me for what I believe will be a profitable journey for you.

"I was out in the backyard and noticed Spotty making a great commotion in front of a tree. I thought it must be a squirrel and went to investigate. It was a scrawny, tiny kitty! . . . It had survived the streets of Austin and ended up in a tree in the only backyard for miles; the backyard of the Governor's mansion. It had little paws that looked like baseball gloves, and it had six toes! . . . we called it Ernie, because Ernest Hemmingway had six-toed cats. I tell kids that the lesson of Ernie is 'No matter what tough circumstances you find yourselves in, never give up. Ernie went from the streets to the Governor's mansion all because a dog chased him into a tree.'" (p. 89, *A Charge To Keep*.)

There's a line we've heard: "When the going gets tough, the tough get going." One thing for sure: You can't tell what's inside a person by what you see on the outside. A reporter once asked Laura Bush if she had lost her voice or felt overshadowed by being near the limelight of her husband's politics so much. She and her husband both agreed: "On the contrary, she found her voice; a powerful voice for reading and literacy, for authors and artists,.." (Ibid. p 92). Laura also shares her husband's conviction that, together, they have an opportunity to help change the direction of the country. They believe that America is at a *critical* time in history—that our country's most urgent need is *spiritual*—not economic.

While we're on the subject of tenacity in trying times let me share a typical quote from First Lady Barbara Bush I found (page 4, Ibid.) the morning after her husband lost the presidential election to Bill Clinton she said: "Well, now, that's behind us. It's time to move on." Doesn't that sound just like her?

Those who knew George W. well thought they saw a lot of change in him from his college years and the time he decided to enter politics. I think so too. He says it quite well for himself. Let's start by quotes from pages 136 to 139:

"Actually, the seeds of my decision had been planted the year before, by the Reverend Billy Graham. He visited my family for a summer weekend in Maine. I saw him preach at the small summer church, St. Ann's by the Sea. We all had lunch on the patio overlooking the ocean. One evening my Dad asked Billy to answer questions from a big group of family gathered for the weekend. He sat by the fire and talked. And what he said sparked a *change* in my heart. I don't remember the exact words. It was more the power of his example. The Lord was so clearly reflected in his gentle and loving demeanor.

"The next day we walked and talked at Walker's Point, and I knew I was in the presence of a great man. *He was like a magnet; I felt drawn to seek something different. He didn't lecture or admonish; he shared warmth and concern. Billy Graham didn't make you feel guilty; he made you feel really loved.*

"Over the course of that weekend, Reverend Graham planted a mustard seed in my soul, a seed that grew over the next year. He led me to the path, and I began walking. And it was the beginning of a change in my life. I had always been a religious person; had regularly attended church, even taught Sunday School and served as an altar boy. But that weekend my faith took on a new meaning. It was the beginning of a new walk where I would re-commit my heart to Jesus Christ.

"I was humbled to learn that God sent His Son to die for a sinner like me. I was comforted to know that through the Son, I could find God's amazing grace, a grace that crosses every border, every barrier and is open to everyone. Through the love of Christ's life, I could understand *the life-changing powers of faith.*

"When I returned to Midland, I began reading the Bible regularly. Don Evans talked me into joining him and another friend, Don Jones, at a men's community Bible study. The group had first assembled the year before, in the Spring of 1984 at the beginning of the downturn in the energy industry.

"Midland was hurting. A lot of people were looking for comfort and strength and direction. A couple men started the Bible study as a support group, and it grew. By the time I began attending, in the fall of

1985, almost 120 men would gather. We met in small groups often and would then join the larger group for full meetings.

"Don Jones picked me up for the meetings. I remember looking forward to them. My interest in reading the Bible grew stronger and stronger. And the words became clearer and more meaningful. We studied Acts, the story of the apostles building the Christian Church, and the next year the Gospel of Luke.

The preparation for each meeting took several hours reading the Scripture passages and thinking through responses to discussion questions. I took it seriously—with my usual touch of humor.

"Laura and I were active members of First Methodist Church of Midland and we participated in many family programs, including James Dobson's Focus on the Family series on raising children. As I studied and learned, Scripture took on greater meaning; I gained confidence and understanding in my faith. I read the Bible regularly. Don Evans gave me the 'One-year Bible' which was divided into 365 daily readings, each one including a section from the New Testament, the Old Testament, Psalms and Proverbs. I read through that Bible every other year. During the years in between I pick out different chapters to study . . .

"I have also learned the power of prayer. I pray for guidance. I do not pray for earthly things, but for heavenly things, like wisdom, patience and understanding.

"My faith gives me focus and perspective. It teaches humility. But I also recognize that faith can be *misinterpreted* in the political process. Faith is an important part of my life. I believe it is important to *live* my faith, not *flaunt* it.

"America is a great country because of our religious freedoms. It is important for any leader to respect the faith of others. That point was driven home when Laura and I visited Israel in 1998. We had traveled to Rome to spend Thanksgiving with our daughter, who was attending a school program there, and we spent three days in Israel on the way home. It was an incredible experience. I remember waking up at the Jerusalem Hilton, opening the curtains and seeing the Old City before us, the Jerusalem stone glowing gold.

We visited the Western Wall, and the Church of the Holy Sepulcher. And we went to the Sea of Galileo and stood atop the hill where Jesus delivered the Sermon on the Mount. It was an overwhelming feeling to stand on the spot where *the most famous speech in the history of the world was delivered*, the place where Jesus outlined the *character* and *conduct* of a "believer" and gave his disciples-and the world—the Beatitudes, the Golden Rule, and the Lord's Prayer.

"Our delegation included four gentile governors—one Methodist, two Catholics and a Mormon; and several Jewish-American friends. Someone suggested we read Scripture. I chose to read 'Amazing Grace,' my favorite hymn.

"Later that night we all gathered at a restaurant in Tel Aviv for dinner before we boarded our middle-of-night flight back to America.

We talked about the wonderful experiences and thanked our guides and government officials who had introduced us to their country. Toward the end of the meal one of our friends rose to share a story; to tell us how he, a gentile, and his friend, a Jew, had (unbeknownst to the rest of us) walked down to the Sea of Galilee, joined hands underwater and prayed together on bended knee. Then out of his mouth came a hymn he had known as a child—*a hymn he had not thought of in years*. He got every word right:

"Now is the time approaching
by prophets long foretold,
When all shall dwell together,
One Shepherd and one fold.
Now Jew and Gentile, meeting,
from many a distant shore,
Around an altar kneeling,
One common Lord adore."

"Faith changes lives. I know, because faith has changed mine."

(Ibid pp 136–139)

To view more of the "mature man" George W. Bush, let me take you back to the middle of page six:

"I could not be Governor if I did not believe in a divine plan that supersedes all human plans. Politics is a fickle business. Polls change. Today's friend may be tomorrow's adversary. People may lavish praise and attention. Many times it is genuine; sometimes it is not. Yet I choose to build my life on a foundation that will not shift. My faith frees me. Frees me to put the problem of the moment in the proper perspective. Frees me to make decisions that others might not like. Frees me to try to do the right thing even though it may not poll well . . ."

(Ibid. p. 6).

Living by Polls or Principles?

When you hear anyone say, "I don't care what anyone else thinks" you can be assured they're a liar or just don't know what they are saying. All normal people are social creatures, and most of what we do and say is because we want the approval/disapproval (or the attention) of other people! Since that is true, everyone in public office is affected by opinion polls! You can divide public servants into two classes: 1) Politicians and 2) Statesmen/Stateswomen. Those in category one think and plan what they do and say around opinion polls. Those in group two choose to build their lives and plans on principles. Yes, they want to know what others think. Yes, they listen when others speak. But they think more of what is right and wrong and beneficial to people they were elected to serve (in the long haul) than they do about what anyone else thinks. They do not allow *their own ego* to rule their thoughts and actions.

Making Difficult Choices

With that in mind, let me urge every thinking person among you who read these lines to ponder and weigh carefully what George W. Bush has to say in chapter eleven of, *A Charge To Keep*. If you don't have a copy of the book, I urge you to get one-even if you have to sell the old red rooster to do it. Anyone who has thought, debated, or wrestled with the idea of capital punishment knows having an issue like that to decide can be a *nightmare* for a head of state, or of a nation. Since I can't reprint the book and give it to you, let me stir your mind to think about a few issues that should really matter to you and your family. The death penalty is one of them. Start with me, J R B, on p. 147 at the first paragraph:

"The death penalty is a difficult issue for supporters as well as its opponents. I have a reverence for life; my faith teaches that life is a gift from our Creator. In a perfect world, life is given by God and only taken by God. I hope someday our society will respect life, the full spectrum of life, from the unborn to the elderly. I hope someday unborn children will be protected by law and welcomed in life. I support the death penalty because I believe, if administered swiftly and justly, capital punishment is a deterrent against future violence and will save other innocent lives. Some advocates of life will challenge why I oppose abortion yet support the death penalty; to me, it's the difference between innocence and guilt.

"Two days before Karla Faye Tucker's scheduled execution, one of my own daughters, obviously troubled by this case, looked up at the dinner table and told me she had decided she opposes capital punishment. I told her I was proud that she was thinking about the issue, that she had a *right* and a *responsibility* to make her own judgment, and she should always feel free to express her opinion. I welcomed the moment. Current events are great teachers . . . As a dad who was also Governor, it made my heart a little heavier, knowing I might have to carry out a sentence with which my own daughter disagreed." Among other things, Mr. Bush went on to explain the above "preventive" rationale, besides his pledge to faithfully uphold and carry out the laws of the state of Texas. (Ibid. p. 147, most of the page!)

Starved for Leadership

Come with me and let's quietly slip into a church in Austin, Texas, and listen to what the newly-elected Governor described:

"Today, two weeks after Jeb's inauguration, in the church in downtown Austin, the pastor, Mark Craig, was telling me that my re-election as the first Governor to win back-to-back four-year terms in the history of the state of Texas was a beginning, not an end—People are starved for *faithfulness*. He talked of the need for honesty in government; he warned that leaders who cheat on their wives will cheat their country, will cheat their colleagues, will cheat themselves. The minister said that America is starved for honest leaders. He told the story of Moses, asked by God to lead his people to a land of milk and honey. Moses had a lot of reasons to shirk the task. As the pastor told it, Moses' basic reaction was, 'Sorry, God, I'm busy. I've got a family. I've got sheep to tend. I've got a life. Who am I that I should go to Pharaoh, and bring the sons of Israel out of Egypt? The people won't believe me . . . I'm not a good speaker. Oh, my Lord, send, I pray, someone else! Moses pleaded. But God did not, and Moses ultimately did his bidding, leading his people through forty years of wilderness wandering, relying on God for strength, direction and inspiration. People are 'starved for leadership' Pastor Craig said, 'starved for leaders who have ethical and moral courage.

"It is not enough to have an ethical compass to know right from wrong. America needs leaders who have the moral courage to do what is right for the right reason. It's not always easy or convenient for leaders to step forward; remember, even Moses had doubts."

"He was talking to you," my mother later said. The pastor was, of course, talking to all of us—challenging each of us to make the most of our lives . . . He was calling on us to use whatever power we have-in business, politics, in our communities, and in our families to do good for the right reason." (Ibid. p.9).

Who Will Go?

Asked if by any chance this might have been the moment of decision in his own mind and heart about running for the presidency, he writes (p. 225):

"There was no "magic moment" of decision. After talking with my family during the Christmas holidays, then hearing the rousing sermon to make the most of every moment during my inaugural church service, I gradually felt more comfortable with the prospect of a presidential campaign. My family would love me, my faith would sustain me, no matter what. During the more than half century of my life, we have seen an unprecented decay in our American culture-a decay that has eroded the foundations of our collective values and moral standards of conduct. Our sense of personal responsibility has declined dramatically, just as the role and responsibility of the federal government have increased. The changing culture blurred the sharp contrast between right and wrong and created a new standard of conduct: 'If it feels good, do it" and "If you've got a problem, blame somebody else." . . . "We're all victims of forces beyond our control." We went from a culture of sacrifice and saving to a culture obsessed with grabbing all, with gusto . . . We went from accepting responsibility to assigning blame.

"As government did more and more, individuals were required to do less and less. The new culture said that if people were poor, the government should feed them. If someone had no house, the government should provide one. If criminals are not responsible for their acts, then the answers are not not in prisons, but social programs . . .

"For our culture to change, it must change one heart, one soul, and one conscience at a time. Government can spend money, but it cannot put hope in our hearts, or a sense of purpose in our lives. (Ibid. p.232)

"But government should welcome the active involvement of people who are following a religious imperative to love their neighbors through after-school programs, child care, drug treatment, maternity group homes, and a range of other services. Supporting these men and women—the soldiers in the armies of compassion—is the next bold step of welfare reform, because I know that changing hearts will change our entire society."

"During the opening months of my presidential campaign, I have traveled our country and my heart has been warmed. My experiences have reinvigorated my faith in the greatness of Americans. They have reminded me that societies are renewed from the bottom up, not from the top down. Everywhere I go I see people of love and faith, taking time to help a neighbor in need. These people, and thousands like them, are the heart and soul and the greatness of America." (Ibid. p.242, par. 2)

"And I want to do my part . . . *I believe America must seize this moment; America must lead. We must give our prosperity greater purpose, a purpose of peace and freedom and hope. We are a great nation of good and loving people. And together, we have a charge to keep.*" (Ibid. p. 243, paragraph 2.)

So said and so wrote George W. Bush, one of our presidential candidates more than two years ago. It seems that I now hear a great throng of Americans answering, "Count me in on that, Mr. President! I'm only one, but all that one I give to be used of God to bring hope and help to the beloved land I have come to love and the world God so loves . . . !"

Please join me in expressing our THANKS to Harper Collins Publishers 10 East 53rd Street, New York, N. Y. 1002-5299, for permission to use the extensive quotes from a timely book in a crucial hour in American history! I urge you to buy the book "A Charge To Keep" and read it all!

Sincerely,
John Robert Boggs, Jr.

P.S. Remember: "The opportunity of a lifetime must be seized in the lifetime of the opportunity."—JRB

24

From the Diary

of An Alzheimer's Caregiver

"A Helping, Healing Touch"

—J. Robert Boggs, Jr.

09/07/89 Winona Lake, IN., Grace Village Health Care
We watched the evening news in the nursing home lounge near the nurses' station. Turning to my wife, a victim of ADRD (Alzheimer's disease or Related Disorders) I said to her: "Well, Sweetheart, I need to get to my apartment and address book orders. Here's your 'good night' kiss. See you in the morning."

With that I gave her a kiss, lingered to give her a loving pat on the shoulder, then turned to leave. I had taken only two steps when someone yelled, **"Hey!"** at me. Whirling around I saw Dr. Gordon sitting close by, stretching his arm toward me.

I grabbed his outstretched hand as I stepped closer to him, and said: "Yes, my friend, how are you?"

He blurted out what I thought was, "Did you touch me?" I was about to say it couldn't have been I who touched him, since I was ten feet away. Suddenly I realized that he had asked, "*Will* you touch me?"

Searching my face with his weak eyes he queried: "You have touched me before, haven't you?"

"Certainly, Dr. Gordon! I have touched you many times. We often shake hands, walk down the hall together, and yes, I have touched you on the shoulder too."

He was asking that I stop by with a *caring touch* on the shoulder for *him* as I left the room, as I had done to Maxine! What a beautiful little request—made with such uninhibited, child-like honesty. What a privilege it was for me to "be there" for him with a caring touch when he needed it.

Dr. Gordon* is one of the newest residents at the Nursing Center. He and his wife, Millie, are both there, in separate rooms, since she is too weak now to contend with his mental confusion. He is about 80 and she is not far behind. They are classic examples of what happens to about 47% of us if we live to be 85. The Gordon's live on the same hall in separate rooms and eat at different tables in the same dining room—for the aforesaid reason. Having been married to Millie for almost sixty years. Dr. Gordon, for the first month there, was very reluctant to sit down to a meal without her. He began to lose weight, which caused all of us closely associated with them to "close ranks" in helping them to adjust to their new situation. But adjust they have, gradually. The many *short* visits by family and close friends during the first month was *crucial* to their adjustment. (And please, family and friends should not forget to pay regular visits afterwards also.)

Though the chance for the average of us to have ADRD is only about 16%, those who live to be 85 and up will find the chance increasing to almost 50%! It is the fourth leading cause of death in America. Heart disease, cancer and strokes are the leading three causes.

Feeding my wife two meals a day for many years afforded a close observation point to watch the human drama as ADRD "did its thing" on its victims. Dr. Gordon

*Not the doctor's real name.

is just one of the more than four million. These people still have feelings and human yearnings like the rest of us. With millions of their brain cells dying daily and the nerves unable to transmit messages normally, the victims cannot properly express the emotions they feel. But be sure they are still there!

Dr. Gordon's request for a touch made me wonder: "How many people within our reach are crying out inside for *a caring touch* from someone? Who will be there to give it? You maybe? Why not!

J. Robert Boggs

Lonely In A Festive Crowd

—J. ROBERT BOGGS

12/17, 1998. I stopped to shop in one of these "mega" stores. The place was festive and beautiful! Even the fresh foods display was done with real finesse and imagination. Everything I saw suggested family, fun, and the joys of the season. I said to myself, "I don't recall *ever* seeing a store of any kind so well decorated."

But the tasteful de'cor and beauty only added to my hurting and loneliness as I pushed my shopping cart slowly down the aisle, blinking in order to see through my tears. My sweetheart-wife and I have had so much joy shopping together for clothes, groceries or whatever. She was a "fun" person to be with anywhere, any time. Now in a nursing home, she is bedfast and blind-in the last stages of Alzheimer's.

Early this morning I had a horrible dream. My Sweetheart was having eye surgery without anesthetic! She was screaming so horribly and pitifully that I have been close to tears all day. The bad dream made me wonder what pain the glaucoma may yet be causing as she suffers so sweetly and silently.

The agony in my heart has continued all day-alongside the joys, sights and sounds of holiday preparations. I suppose the hurting will keep on as long as she lives and suffers. Real love is like that, they say. Loneliness is difficult to combat. It sneaks up on you even when you're in a happy crowd. It can hit you when you are contentedly alone.

Having no brothers, I learned early to like solitude at times. But not *this* much! The wise words of the Creator in Genesis 2:18, "It is not good for the man to be alone" I find meaningful. Our daughters and their families have been wonderfully helpful. But they have their own lives to live and children to enjoy. I love them too much to ask any more of them.

Therefore, I purpose in my heart to quietly cope with whatever degree of loneliness is mine by:

1) Joining the recreation and other activities at the retirement village where I live.

2) Watching for others who may be hurting inside, seeking ways to sincerely cheer them on-just as I would appreciate others boosting me when I'm a bit down.

3) Let each little "surprise visit" of loneliness prod me to remember that many of my happiest moments I now recall as such are ones that I did not recognize *at the time.*

4) I will try to be aware of the significance of each happening, lest by default, I carelessly neglect to say "thank you" to all those who help create the *joy of the moment.* I especially want to cultivate the attitude of gratitude to The Father of All Mercies for the *JOYS* that keep coming, flowing endlessly, no matter what!

—JRB

Diary of An Alzheimer's Caregiver
"I'll Move Over!"

—J. Robert Boggs

12/20/87 Warsaw. IN . . .

Our stroll In the halls was over. My wife, Maxine, was tucked into bed at 9:00 p.m.

"Let me kiss you good night. Sweetheart. It's time for me to head over to my little apartment."

"Oh, please don't leave me. Honey! You don't have to go back to Grace Village tonight. Just stay here with me." To her it sounded so reasonable; so simple and easy.

"How I wish we could stay together. Sweetheart!" I assured her. "But I doubt if your room-mate would approve."

"Oh. It would be O.K. with you, wouldn't it Mabel?" Mabel was silent. (Which does not always "give consent.")

"But Sweetheart, even if Mabel didn't mind, the nurse would come In shortly and boot me out."

"Oh, no she wouldn't! She wouldn't mind at all. Honey please!—just stay right here with me tonight!"

With my heart doing strange things inside me, I took a deep breath and said slowly: "Sweetheart, even if Mabel did not mind, nor the nurse object, I still couldn't stay here. Where would I sleep?"

"Right here with me." Looking from her beautiful, pleading eyes to the single hospital bed, I replied:

"I'm afraid there isn't enough room on that one little bed for the two of us."

"Oh, sure there is! *I'LL MOVE OVER!*"

What a spirit! What an attitude! So ready to "adjust" with no thought of any inconvenience to herself. With AD (Alzheimer's Disease) slowly destroying her brain, the reasoning was faulty, but what a *heart of love!* Without wavering she showed that attitude for more than sixteen years of our struggle is AD! Many patients get downright mean, but Maxine never did. What a miracle of God's great grace! The prophet's words (Nehemiah 8:10) "The joy of the Lord is your strength" seemed to fit in my life all those long years and made them wonderful, "in spite of" difficult times!

Out of deep gratitude to God I published my first book in 1994 entitled, *"I'LL MOVE OVER—The Story of a Great Love."* It sold more than 6,000 copies, and took me on some speaking tours for a few years. As Alzheimer's began the last stages, I began to ask our Lord to please not let me be gone when my "Maxine" went *Home.* Six years later, on May 22, 2000 about 9:00 p.m., after only a few days of a near coma stage, both of our daughters and I, plus one of our sons-in-law, were beside her bed when she breathed her last. We were all there to give her the most *joyful,* howbeit tearful, sendoff you can imagine!

A few days later the large Grace Village Chapel was full of people from "all over" with tributes to this delightful lady who had graced our parsonages and given away thousands of happy smiles to people for her long, genuinely good life!

The next year my deep loneliness was ended by God's gracious gift of another beautiful Christian companion for this lonely old fellow people say looks much younger! You have read about Jodie already in Chapter 20. God's *best* to every one of your familyl!

Astronaut Rick Husband's Final Flight

—J. ROBERT BOGGS

02/01/03

At 9:00 a.m. on February 1, we waited on the runway at Indianapolis for our plane to be de-iced, unaware that the space shuttle *COLUMBIA* exploded while we sat there, as it re-entered the earth's atmosphere and was streaking over eastern Texas toward western Louisiana. The captain of the craft, Rick Husband and the six others of the crew, plummeted to the earth along with the scraps of the spacecraft. Condolences and expressions of grief poured into America from all over the world-except the Muslim parts. Their vindictive messages with TV pictures of dancing, celebration and joy was in sharp contrast. I reject the urge to comment further on reactions like that, lest I bring God's promised judgment on myself that His enemies will get! That is what our Bible says will happen if we rejoice at the calamity of our enemies. I might add that Jesus commanded us to *love* people, even our personal enemies, and to pray for those who hate us and treat us with spite.

You may not know that Rick Husband was very fond of Steve Green's music and singing. He and his wife Evelyn were waiting in line some years ago to thank Steve for his concert. Steve's wife whispered to him that the next fellow in line was an astronaut. Steve "made a big deal about it" he later said, "and pretty soon the line turned and started to wait in line to get *his* signature instead of mine!"

Steve Green was present for Rick's first shuttle launch some time later. He was also at this last one, and sang both times at pre-launch receptions. Steve said the last reception was "very Christ-honoring," and there were many unbelievers present. Steve described Rich as a quiet, unassuming man who was, however, very vocal about his Christian faith. He said that Rick did not miss a chance to give glory to God and mentioned that when Mission Control said it was a beautiful day for a launch, Rick answered with, "The Lord has given us a perfect day!"

A suit technician shared with Steve this story: "After the astronauts suit up they walk down a hallway. Then they were about to open a door to face the press. Rick stopped the crew before they opened the door and said he wanted to pray with them. The technicians later talked about it. One said that in all his years he had never heard of a captain praying for and with his crew!

The spouses of the crew each get to pick a song for them to wake up to one of the mornings they're in space. Rick's wife selected "God of Wonders" by Steve Green. Steve played a tape for us of Rick communicating with Mission Control after the after the song was played. The conversation went something like this: Mission Control—"Good morning. That song was for Rick. It was 'God of Wonders' by Steve Green." Rick-"Good morning. Thank you. We can really appreciate the lyrics of that song up here. We look out the window and see that God truly is a God of wonders!" Steve also shared part of an e-mail he got from Rick, from outer space! He wrote about how overwhelming it was to see God's vast creation from space. He said he had never cried while exercising before, but pedaling on the bike and looking out the window at God's incredible creation brought tears to his eyes.

While *Columbia* and crew were in flight, Steve Green had a concert at which the families of Rick Husband and Mike Anderson were asked to stand while the audience joined Steve in praying for their spouses. He remarked that there were at least three Christians in the spacecraft. Steve also shared that with President George W. Bush, where he met to comfort the families, joined with them in a circle and prayed for them.

Rick Husband took parenting seriously. Before he left on the *Columbia* he made 34 devotionals, by video. Seventeen for his daughter and 17 for his son, one for each day he was to be gone. That way both his children could have their regular devotionals with "Daddy" while he was gone. What treasures they will be to the son and daughter the rest of their lives! Which prods me to ask myself and you: What valuable "treasures" are we leaving with our children they will cherish and value when we are gone?

Yes, God really *is* at work in His world! He gave us a beautiful and perfect world. God then gave us freedom of choice, and, unfortunately, we miss-used that freedom and messed up the beautiful world and ourselves too. But God took on the project: "Operation Restoration" and asks our cooperation and help. How are you doing with your part in the recovery project?

Appendix

Photo Section

FORGIVENESS

Forgiveness is a gift,
to the one who forgives;
Seventy times seven,
for as long as one lives.
Forgiveness means pardon,
ourselves and our brothers;
We, when free from our guilt
exonerate others.
We practice it daily,
hoping to attain it;
With repeated action
needed to sustain it.
The Master teaches us
in His own love letters;
We, to be forgiven,
must forgive our debtors.
When we have made the choice,
forgiveness brings release;
Our hearts always rejoice,
rewarded by real peace.

—martha l. schaffer

"Bill" Massengale & little Donna

Anthony "Tony" Vigna

LIVING BY FAITH

Our heav'nly Father tells us that
By faith we must so live;
Do not depend on how we feel,
For pitfalls it will give.
We can abide within His fold
If we believe we can;
He walks along close by our side
And takes us by the hand.
He bends down low to listen to
His children's humble plea;
And when the answer does appear,
*Faith is **reality**.*
His holiness and beauty rare
In trust we can behold;
His glory is so much more vast
Than ever can be told.
In Him we place our confidence
Again each day anew;
As we believe, our faith will grow,
And it will see us through.

©—Martha L. Schaffer—

Judy & Bill Osborne

MY PRAYER

Lord, lead me in the path
you'd have me to go;
Teach me eternal truth
you'd have me to know.
Give me the proper words
you'd have me to speak;
Kind, softly uttered ones,
both humble and meek.
Before me keep in view
your will understood;
My ways to make anew
when change is for good.
Let every conscious thought
be noble and pure;
Wherein my plans are wrought,
born, grow and mature.
Lord, let me understand,
tho' misunderstood;
And lend a helping hand,
as only love could.
Your presence, my heart asks
to be made aware;
While fulfilling my tasks
in your love and care.

©—martha l. schaffer

Donna Massengale with
Melvin, Ricky, & Gary.

Tony Vigna's last Pastorate in S. Bend IN

Wm. Mercer Massengale 1943

across a lake and then walked 2 miles in the woods to the marsh where we cut the hay with a sythe and we coiled it up & then we carried it to where we stacked it up, the stack was 12 or 15 ft. high. We hauled it out through the woods & down the lake on the ice, pretty good feed for the horses!

Russel W. Smith

On our farm we tapped 50 trees (these were hard maples) around the 1st of April when the weather was (?) & temp above freezing. The sap would run; we boiled it down to syrup in a big iron kettle. It was later made into sugar on the kitchen stove, the syrup was stored in bottles or cans.

"Oh" my house is burning!   —R.W. Smith

In Equador, in 1956, when the five young American
Christian missionaries were speared by the Aucas
(Waodonis) by their six men, other tribe members
watched in hiding. They later revealed what they saw—
a multitude of people in the treetops, dressed in white,
also watching! God watches his own!

Alice and I are in the sunset years of our lives now; we both look back on a good life. We are enjoying life together, God has blessed us with good families and good health.

Russel W. Smith

LIGHT UP YOUR CORNER

Light up the corner where you are,
it's a needed, important place;
A loving God has placed you there
for you to run a zealous race.
Think not that all is beautiful,
if from the woeful times you're spared;
We know that many varied kinds
of stressful burdens all have shared.
So much depends on **attitude**
toward what one may face in life;
A grateful heart strive to maintain,
and you will never dwell on strife.
Light up the corner where you are,
and make it a delightful place;
Count all your blessings and you'll find
a brilliant glow is on your face.

©—Martha L. Schaffer

"Bill" & Ruth Massengale happy young couple 1941

WE NEED YOU, LORD

*AS WE WALK DOWN LIFE'S
VARIED WAYS,
IN THIS NEW YEAR, LORD,
GIFT FROM YOU;
WE NEED YOUR GUIDANCE ALL
OUR DAYS,
AND STRENGTH YOU PROMISED
TO RENEW.
WE NEED THIS YEAR MORE
THAN BEFORE
TO SEEK, TO FIND, AND KNOW
YOUR WILL,
TO STRIVE TO PLEASE AND
FOLLOW YOU,
AND TRULY YOUR DESIRES
FULFILL.*

©—*martha l. schaffer*

CHOICES

THERE ARE FIRM CHOICES I MUST MAKE,
EACH DAWNING OF THE SUN;
FOR THEY WILL MAKE A DIFFERENCE WHEN
THE TOIL OF DAY IS DONE.
I NEED TO ASK DIRECTION THAT
I ALWAYS DO MY PART;
AND PRAY THAT CHOICES MADE ARE FROM
AN HONEST, OPEN HEART.
I MAKE THE CHOICE TO CLOSE MY MIND
OR OPEN IT TO LIGHT;
WITH CONSTANT RAYS OF GUIDANCE TO
DISCERNMENT AND INSIGHT.
IN FAITH I ASK AND THEN PROCEED
TO HEAR A SILENT VOICE;
"NOT EVERYTHING JUST HAPPENS FOR
IN LIFE, MUCH COMES BY CHOICE."

©—martha l. schaffer

SECURITY

WHEN I AM WEARY, DOWN AND OUT,
AND FEEL I CAN NOT COPE;
I LOOK TO MY DEAR SAVIOUR AND
HE COMES TO ME WITH HOPE.
WHEN LIFE'S ROAD SEEMS SO DREARY AS
I'M GROPING IN THE NIGHT,
HE WHISPERS, "LOOK THIS WAY, MY CHILD,"
AND LEADS ME TO THE LIGHT.
HE HEARS THE PLEA OF MY VEXED SOUL,
AND ANSWERS WHEN I CALL;
HE HOLDS ME SAFELY IN HIS ARMS,
TO NEVER LET ME FALL.
HE COMFORTS ME WITH PEACE AND JOY,
THE WORLD CAN NEVER GIVE;
AND BRINGS TO MIND HIS PROMISE TO
"COME UNTO ME AND LIVE."

—martha l. schaffer

THANK YOU, MY FRIEND

THANK YOU FOR LENDING ME YOUR FAITH
WHEN MINE IS WEAK AND ALMOST GONE;
IN HEART AND SOUL YOU'VE FELT MY PAIN,
I'M GRATEFUL FOR THE GOOD YOU'VE DONE.
I NEED YOUR HOPE ALONG WITH FAITH,
THAT I, MY DUTIES MAY FULFILL;
AND TRUST, WHEN I, NO HOPE CAN SEE,
TO DO MY BEST TO FIND GOD'S WILL.
YOUR PRAYERS IN MY BEHALF I SENSE,
THEY LIFT ME UP WHEN I AM LOW;
YOUR CHEERFUL WORDS LIGHT UP MY PATH
TO GIVE ME COURAGE . . . THAT WILL GROW.
I THANK YOU FOR FAITH, HOPE AND LOVE,
THE KIND TRUE FRIENDS WILL SURELY GIVE;
THEY RADIATE WITHIN YOUR SMILE,
REFLECTIONS OF THE WAY YOU LIVE.

—martha l. schaffer

THE AFTERGLOW

GOD SENDS THE RAIN, TRANSPARENT, PURE
ON SHADES OF EARTHY HUE,
NO HUMAN PLAN APPEARS MATURE
WHEN HIS PLAN COMES IN VIEW.
CLEAR CRYSTAL BEADS THRIVE AND ABOUND
TO BATHE THE THIRSTY EARTH,
THEY CLEANSE THE AIR; SUSTAIN THE GROUND
AND BRING TO LIFE NEW BIRTH.
THE PEACEFUL PATTER ON THE ROOF,
SO TRANQUIL AND SERENE
REVEALS TO MAN SUCH SIMPLE TRUTH,
GOD'S OWN DESIGN SUPREME.
TRANSCENDENT WONDERS GOD HAS WROUGHT,
HIS IMAGE TO BESTOW;
TO EVERY SEASON HE HAS BROUGHT
HIS RADIANT AFTERGLOW.

©—martha l. schaffer

CLAY IN YOUR HANDS

MAKE ME IN YOUR HANDS, DEAR LORD,
AS CLAY IN THE POTTER'S HAND;
SHAPE MY LIFE INTO YOUR WILL,
WHILE CHANGING AT YOUR COMMAND.
KEEP ME PLIABLE, DEAR LORD,
REDUCING TO CLAY ONCE MORE;
RE-FORM AGAIN AND AGAIN,
TO YOUR PERFECTION RESTORE.
REMOLD ME, LORD, AS NEEDED,
CREATE THE PATTERN YOU CHOOSE;
LET EMERGE FROM THE POTTER'S WHEEL,
A VESSEL YOU CAN USE.

©—martha l. schaffer